CHALET
ARCHITECTURE + DESIGN

MASTERPIECES

MICHELLE GALINDO

CHALET
ARCHITECTURE + DESIGN

BRAUN

PREFACE. VORWORT. PRÉFACE.

During vacation people want to escape the routine of their everyday lives, a wish that is also reflected in architecture. How do architects from all corners of the globe design the "other living spaces" that are used during vacation? One option consists of prefabricated vacation homes. But these are usually only a simpler form of single-family homes. In contrast, the custom-made chalets in this book with their attractive incorporation of nature and architecture demonstrate the creativity of their designers.

Originally the term "chalet" described a simple herder hut in the Swiss Alps. The term is derived from the Indo-European root "cala" meaning "shelter." The typical style of a chalet is a cubic structure with dark wood timbering and an overhanging gable roof. Initially shelters for herders, today's chalets all around the world are retreats for city dwellers seeking to escape the bustle of their daily lives. In addition to the typical Swiss wooden buildings, the American tradition of cabins or lodges also influenced the design of contemporary chalets. At their core, the new interpretations of both earlier forms are based on the same premises – regional styles are combined with modern structures. As opposed to city buildings, however, the designs are not matched to the architecture of the surrounding buildings but to the topography of the landscape.

In den Ferien wollen wir aus der Routine des Alltags ausbrechen. Ein Wunsch, der sich auch in der Architektur widerspiegelt. Wie gestalten Architekten rund um den Globus das „andere Wohnen" im Urlaub? Eine Möglichkeit sind Ferienhäuser in Fertigbauweise. Doch sie sind zumeist nur einfachere Versionen des Einfamilienhauses. Die maßgeschneiderten Chalets in diesem Band hingegen zeugen in ihrer reizvollen Spannung zwischen Natur und Baukunst von der Kreativität ihrer Baumeister.

Ursprünglich bezeichnete der Begriff „Chalet" eine einfache Sennhütte in den Schweizer Alpen. Der Ausdruck ist vom präromanischen „cala" abgeleitet und bedeutet „Schutz". Die typische Erscheinungsform ist ein kubischer Baukörper mit dunkler Holzverschalung und auskragendem Satteldach. Während hier einst Hirten Unterschlupf fanden, ist das Chalet heute ein Rückzugsort für Städter, die der Hektik des Alltags entfliehen wollen. Und das in aller Welt. Neben dem klassischen Schweizer Holzbau ist somit auch die amerikanische Tradition der „Cabin" oder „Lodge" in die Gestaltung des zeitgenössischen Chalets eingeflossen. Im Kern verfolgen die Neu-Interpretationen beider Vorläufer dieselben Grundsätze: Regionale Typologien werden mit moderner Formsprache kombiniert. Anders als in der Stadt orientieren sich die Entwürfe dabei nicht

Les vacances nous permettent de rompre la monotonie du quotidien et les maisons dans lesquelles nous les passons jouent ici un rôle déterminant. Mais comment les architectes de différents pays conçoivent-ils les « maisons de vacances » ? Bien que le préfabriqué constitue une réponse, il reproduit souvent, dans une version « light », l'esthétique des pavillons de banlieue. Les chalets sur mesure présentés dans cet ouvrage illustrent par contre la créativité des architectes lorsqu'il s'agit de jouer sur le contraste entre nature et habitat.

Le mot « chalet » (du romanche « cala », c'est-à-dire « abri ») s'appliquait à l'origine à des refuges des Alpes suisses. Un chalet typique se présente sous la forme d'un cube en bois sombre, couvert d'un toit à deux pentes très débordant. Hier encore simple abri de berger, le chalet est aujourd'hui une demeure recherchée par les citadins qui souhaitent s'y reposer de leur quotidien trépidant. Du fait de l'internationalisation du modèle, la forme suisse d'origine s'est alliée à la tradition américaine des « lodges » et autres « cabins » pour donner naissance aux chalets contemporains. Ces nouvelles interprétations du thème traditionnel reprennent les mêmes idées de base et associent des éléments régionaux au style moderne. Cependant, contrairement aux édifices urbains, elles cherchent moins à s'harmoniser aux

Whether the project is a skiing lodge in the Alps, the Rocky Mountains, or the Andes, and whether the task takes the architects to Norwegian fjords, Japanese forests or the Australian outback – coping with the impressive natural setting is always a challenge and an opportunity at the same time. For some projects, extreme climatic circumstances limit the time slot for the construction to a few months. The chalet must be able to withstand snow, storm or strong sun. On the other hand, the surrounding nature practically begs to be put in the spotlight. Therefore chalets typically include window openings that frame sections of the scenery like paintings. In addition, panorama windows offer spectacular views and open the chalet up to the outside.

Local wood and natural rock are the predominant materials, sometimes with modern interceptions of concrete, steel and glass. The styles range from the archaic via rustic to modern minimalism. The layouts are defined by clarity and openness. In many chalets, the functional areas of eating, sleeping and living blend into each other, offering families a communicative living experience coupled with maximum space utilization.

The interior furnishings usually focus on the essential. A central fireplace and comfortable sleeping berths are elements of a simple residential environment in front of a breathtaking natural setting – it is the simple things, which turn the "other living quarters" during vacation into a special experience. The luxury is not based on expensive materials or ingenious details, but rather on the unique location of each chalet. This is why the presented designs pay their respect to nature through sustainable building methods and an esthetically appealing style that appreciates and highlights the beauty of the landscape.

an der Architektur umgebender Bauten, sondern an der Topographie der Landschaft.

Egal ob es sich um eine Skihütte in den Alpen, den Rocky Mountains oder den Anden handelt, oder ob die Bauaufgabe die Architekten an norwegische Fjorde, in japanische Wälder oder die australische Einöde führt: Die beeindruckenden Naturkulissen sind Herausforderung und Chance zugleich. Zum Teil beschränken extreme klimatische Bedingungen das Zeitfenster für den Bau auf wenige Monate. Das Chalet muss Schnee, Sturm oder starker Sonneneinstrahlung trotzen. Andererseits verlangt die Natur geradezu danach, in Szene gesetzt zu werden. Charakteristisch sind Fensterluken, die die Umgebung ausschnitthaft einrahmen wie ein Gemälde. Zusätzlich erlauben Panoramafenster spektakuläre Aussichten und öffnen das Chalet nach außen.

Die vorherrschenden Materialien sind Hölzer und Natursteine der jeweiligen Region, zuweilen modern gebrochen durch den Einsatz von Beton, Stahl und Glas. Die stilistische Bandbreite reicht von archaischen über rustikale Formen bis hin zu modernem Minimalismus. Klarheit und Offenheit bestimmen die Grundrisse. In vielen Chalets fließen die funktionalen Bereiche Essen, Schlafen und Wohnen ineinander und bieten den Familien bei maximaler Raumausnutzung ein kommunikatives Wohnerlebnis.

Die Inneneinrichtung konzentriert sich häufig auf das Wesentliche. Ein zentraler Kamin, gemütliche Schlafkojen, eine schlichte Wohnlandschaft vor atemberaubender Naturkulisse – es sind die einfachen Dinge, die das „andere Wohnen" in den Ferien zu einem puren Erlebnis machen. Der Luxus besteht weniger in kostspieligen Materialien oder ausgeklügelten Details, als vielmehr im einzigartigen Standort eines jeden Chalets. Darum zollen die präsentierten Entwürfe der Natur ihren Respekt – durch nachhaltige Bauweise ebenso wie durch eine Ästhetik, die die Schönheit der Landschaft würdigt und unterstreicht.

édifices voisins (absents la plupart du temps) qu'à la topographie et au paysage.

Alpes, Andes ou Montagnes Rocheuses, fjord norvégien, forêt du Japon ou désert australien : l'environnement naturel, souvent de qualité exceptionnelle, est toujours un challenge pour les architectes qui conçoivent un chalet. Notamment parce que des conditions climatiques extrêmes peuvent réduire la période constructible à quelques mois seulement, tandis que la neige, les tempêtes ou un fort ensoleillement imposent des contraintes considérables au bâtiment. D'autre part, l'architecture doit mettre en valeur la nature environnante, principalement au moyen de petites ouvertures qui sont autant de cadres pour le paysage, ou au contraire par des fenêtres panoramiques qui ouvrent le chalet sur l'extérieur et offrent des vues spectaculaires sur les environs.

Les matériaux de construction principaux du chalet restent le bois et la pierre d'origine locale, même s'ils se complètent à l'occasion par le béton, l'acier ou le verre. Quant au style, il va de l'archaïsme aux formes rustiques en passant par le minimalisme moderne. Le plan est majoritairement clair et ouvert : dans de nombreux chalets, le séjour, la salle à manger et les chambres sont étroitement interconnectés, ce qui permet d'optimiser la gestion de l'espace et favorise la communication entre les utilisateurs.

Les aménagements intérieurs se réduisent fréquemment au minimum. Cheminée centrale, couchettes confortables et habitat simple dans un environnement naturel d'une beauté époustouflante contribuent d'une manière décisive à faire des vacances au chalet une aventure inoubliable. Le luxe consiste moins dans l'excellence des matériaux ou l'abondance de détails pratiques, que dans le caractère exceptionnel du site. C'est pourquoi toutes les réalisations présentées dans l'ouvrage témoignent d'un profond respect pour la nature, tant par leur compatibilité avec le développement durable que par leur style en harmonie avec la beauté du paysage environnant.

PROJECTS. PRO

JEKTE. PROJETS.

PACO,
ANYWHERE

JO NAGASAKA + SCHEMATA ARCHITECTURE OFFICE IN PARTNERSHIP WITH E&Y - MIHOKOMORI, SHUHEI NAKAMURA, IZUMI OKAYASU

www.sschemata.com

Client: Roovice, **Completion:** 2009, **Gross floor area:** 6 m², **Photos:** Courtesy of Jo Nagasaka + Schemata Architecture Office.

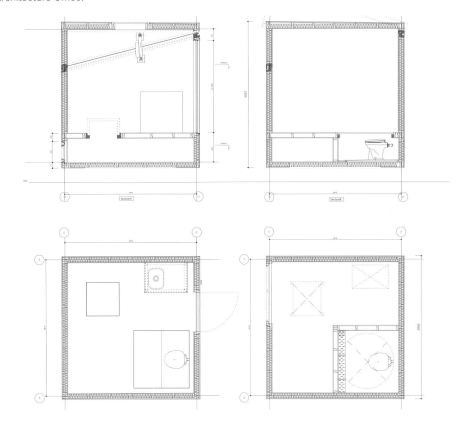

Left: Exterior with beach view. Links: Strandansicht. À gauche: Pavillon sur une plage. | Right: Floor plans. Rechts: Grundrisse. À droite: Plans.

Japanese architects Jo Nagasaka + Schemata Architecture Office have designed a house contained in a three-meter cube. It has the minimum equipment needed to live despite its size. They produced it as a conceptual model to imagine a new lifestyle. "Paco" can be placed in any environment, be it inside a house, a factory or in nature besides oceans and mountains. Intended as a second home, the box has a hinged roof and contains a hammock, desk, sink and shower. Depends on the combination, it describes different lifestyle and landscape.

Die japanischen Architekten Jo Nagasaka + Schemata Architecture Office haben ein Haus entworfen, das in einem Würfel von drei Meter Seitenlänge enthalten ist. Trotzdem verfügt es über die zum Leben notwendige minimale Ausstattung. Paco wurde als neues Wohnkonzept entwickelt. Der Kubus lässt sich überall aufstellen, in einem Haus, einer Fabrik oder in der Natur. Die als Zweitwohnung gedachte Box besitzt ein Klappdach und ist mit einer Hängematte, einem Tisch und einer Dusche ausgerüstet. Abhängig von ihrer Funktion beschreibt sie einen anderen Lebensstil und eine andere Landschaft.

Cette réalisation du bureau japonais Jo Nagasaka + Schemata Architecture Office consiste en un cube dont les arêtes mesurent trois mètres et qui, en dépit de sa taille minimum, contient tous les équipements dont on a besoin pour vivre. Il s'agit d'un pavillon conçu comme un modèle conceptuel pour un nouveau mode de vie, pouvant être placé dans une multitude d'environnements : à l'intérieur d'une maison ou d'une usine, sur une plage ou à la montagne. Équipée d'un hamac, d'un bureau, d'un évier, d'une douche et d'un toit mobile pour l'aération, cette « boîte » est compatible avec une multitude de situations.

From left to right, from above to below:
Sleeping area, washroom, hammock, dinning area.
Right: Beachfront view of exterior.

Von links nach rechts, von oben nach unten:
Schlafraum, Badezimmer, Hängematte, Essecke.
Rechts: Strandansicht.

De gauche à droite, du haut vers le bas:
« caisse à dormir », coin toilette, hamac, coin repas.
À droite: Pavillon sur une plage.

UNDER THE MOONLIGHT HOUSE,
VICTORIA, AUSTRALIA

STUDIO GIOVANNI D'AMBROSIO

www.giovannidambrosio.com
Client: Ray Group, **Completion:** 2007, **Gross floor area:** 340 m², **Photos:** Peter Mylonas.

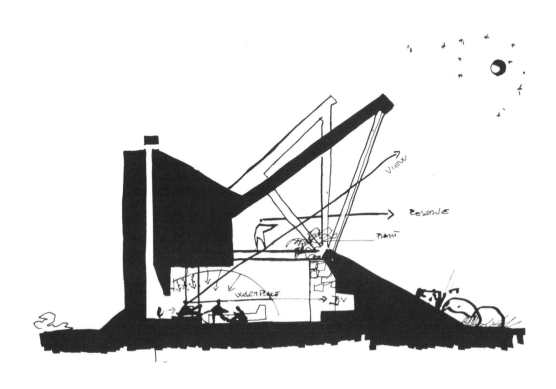

Left: External view. Links: Außenansicht. À gauche: Vue de l'extérieur. | Right: Section. Rechts: Schnitt. À droite: Vue en coupe.

The project tries to integrate itself in the site through use of materials that have been used before and that are part of local historical background. House's shape resembles typological archetypes used by countrymen and cowboys that lived in the area. Stone, wood and metal are materials used for both structure and construction of the project. The House has been designed in order to comfort seasonal stay, both during summer and winter, and lets visitors appreciate the natural environment surrounding them. This has been done through placement of many glazed frames that grant wider external views. On the second level, two bedrooms are included as well as a master bedroom with bathroom and spa.

Mit bereits einmal verwendeten Materialien, die zur örtlichen Geschichte gehören, soll das Gebäude in den Standort eingebunden werden. Die Gestalt des Hauses gleicht den typologischen Urformen, der sich die Farmer und Cowboys dieser Region bedienten. Stein, Holz und Metall sind die vorherrschenden Materialien. Das Haus soll zu jeder Jahreszeit einen angenehmen Aufenthalt bieten, damit Besucher die natürliche Umgebung genießen können. Bewerkstelligt wurde dies durch viele gerahmte Verglasungen, die weiträumigere Aussichten nach draußen gewähren. Auf der zweiten Ebene befinden sich zwei Schlafräume sowie ein Elternschlafzimmer mit Bad und Wellnessbereich.

L'architecte a cherché à intégrer la maison dans son environnement naturel en associant au métal et au verre des matériaux traditionnels tels que la pierre et le bois. La forme du bâtiment s'inspire des constructions traditionnelles locales habitées par des fermiers et des cow-boys. L'édifice, habitable toute l'année, offre de belles vues sur la campagne environnante grâce à de larges baies vitrées. À l'étage se trouvent la chambre du propriétaire, deux chambres d'invités ainsi qu'une salle de bain et d'hydrothérapie.

From left to right, from above to below:
Exterior view, alternative exterior view,
bathroom, living room from above.
Right: Living room with fireplace.

Von links nach rechts, von oben nach unten:
Stein- und Glasfassade, Außenansicht,
Badezimmer, Blick ins Wohnzimmer.
Rechts: Wohnzimmer mit Kamin.

De gauche à droite, du haut vers le bas:
Deux vues de l´extérieur, salle de bains,
séjour vu d'en haut.
À droite: Séjour avec cheminée.

EFH_BATSCHUNS,
BATSCHUNS, AUSTRIA

K_M.ARCHITEKTUR DI DANIEL SAUTER

www.k-m-architektur.com

Client: Private, **Completion:** 2006, **Gross floor area:** 270 m², **Photos:** Daniel Sauter.

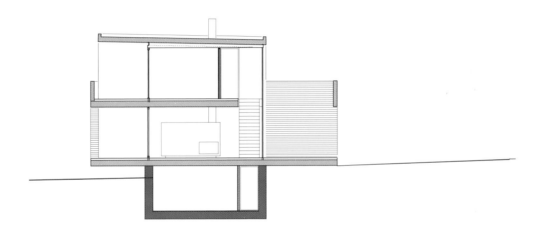

Left: Front view. Links: Vorderansicht. À gauche: Façade principale. | Right: Cross section. Rechts: Querschnitt. À droite: Coupe transversale.

The different functions of the residential home are clearly divided by floors and immediately visible from the outside through the applied façade materials. The upper floor, with a copper plate façade, houses the private bedrooms of the family. The ground floor, covered in larch wood plates, contains an office as well as a generous dining and living space with a stove acting as a room divider. The courtyard-like open terrace to the north offers a view and a sun shield in the summer. Positioned in front of the living area and the kitchen, a roofed terrace, links the interior to the exterior space through room-high glazing.

Die unterschiedlichen Funktionen des Wohnhauses sind klar nach Geschossen getrennt und anhand der verwendeten Fassadenmaterialien deutlich von außen ablesbar. Im Obergeschoß mit Kupferblechfassade befinden sich die privaten Schlafräume der Familie. Im lärchenholzverschalten Erdgeschoss sind ein Büro sowie ein großzügiger Wohn- und Essbereich mit Ofen als Raumteiler untergebracht. Die hofähnliche, nach oben offene Terrasse im Norden bietet Ausblicke und dient im Sommer als Sonnenschutz. Eine dem Wohnraum und der Küche vorgelagerte, überdachte Terrasse verbindet durch die raumhohe Verglasung den Innenraum mit dem Außenraum.

Les différents matériaux utilisés pour la façade reflètent la diversité des pièces dans cette maison sur deux niveaux. Le rez-de-chaussée, où se trouvent un bureau et un grand salon/salle à manger doté d'un poêle qui divise l'espace, a reçu un bardage en planches en mélèze. Quant au niveau supérieur qui abrite les chambres, il est recouvert de plaques de cuivre. La grande terrasse qui s'étend au nord offre un panorama magnifique et reste à l'abri du soleil été comme hiver. Une seconde terrasse, en retrait par rapport au premier étage, s'étire le long de la cuisine et du salon dont le mur, entièrement vitré, assure la liaison entre l'intérieur et l'extérieur.

From left to right, from above to below:
Staircase, exterior view, bathroom.
Right: Dining area.

Von links nach rechts, von oben nach unten:
Treppe ins Obergeschoss, Außenansicht, Küche.
Rechts: Essecke.

De gauche à droite, du haut vers le bas:
Escalier, vue de l'extérieur, salle de bain.
À droite: Salle à manger.

HOUSE AT TUGSTEIN,
DORNBIRN, AUSTRIA

PHILIPP BERKTOLD ARCHITEKT

www.aufderblumenwiese.net
Client: Ingeborg & Dr. Gerhard Thurnher, **Completion:** 2006, **Gross floor area:** 109 m², **Photos:** Robert Fässler.

Left: Entry. Links: Eingang. À gauche: Entrée. | Right: Floor plans. Rechts: Grundrisse. À droite: Plans.

The lower floor of the three-floor single-family house for two persons is made of exposed concrete. This level of the house offers room for two cars, a technical room and the entrance stairs to the two floors with living spaces located above. These levels consist of a wooden construction. The compact light wooden residential structure is positioned on top of a steel concrete frame that opens up towards the valley, providing both a basis for the house as well as a support for the slope. The construction style makes the design visible from the outside through the applied materials. It is accentuated by an unprocessed silver fir wood façade.

Das dreigeschossige Einfamilienhaus für zwei Personen ist im Untergeschoss in massiver Bauweise aus Sichtbeton ausgeführt. Diese Ebene des Hauses bietet Platz für zwei Autounterstellplätze, einen Technikraum und den Ein- beziehungsweise Aufgang zu den darüber liegenden zwei Wohngeschossen. Diese Ebenen sind als konstruktiver Holzbau angelegt. Über einer talseitig offenen Stahlbetonschale, die sowohl zur Gründung des Hauses als auch zur Sicherung des Hanges dient, erhebt sich der kompakte, leichte Wohnkörper aus Holz. Durch diese Bauweise spiegelt die Materialisierung die Art der Konstruktion nach Außen wider. Verstärkt wird diese Erscheinung durch die Fassade aus natur belassener Weißtanne.

Cette maison sur trois niveaux pour deux personnes présente un rez-de-chaussée en béton brut de coffrage qui abrite un garage pour deux voitures, un local technique et un escalier desservant les étages supérieurs. Ce socle en béton ouvert du côté de la vallée, qui sert à la fois de fondations et de renfort contre les glissements de terrain, supporte les deux étages d'habitation réalisés en bois. Ce type de construction reflète un certain enracinement local, encore renforcé par le revêtement en sapin blanc de la façade.

From left to right, from above to below:
Dining area, exterior, fireplace.
Right: Exterior at night.

Von links nach rechts, von oben nach unten:
Essecke, Außenansicht, Kamin.
Rechts: Rückansicht bei Nacht.

De gauche à droite, du haut vers le bas:
Salle à manger, vue de l'extérieur, cheminée.
À droite: La maison au crépuscule.

EFH_EICHENBERG,
EICHENBERG, AUSTRIA

K_M.ARCHITEKTUR DI DANIEL SAUTER

www.k-m-architektur.com

Client: Private, **Completion:** 2005, **Gross floor area:** 370 m², **Photos:** Courtesy of k_m.architektur DI Daniel Sauter.

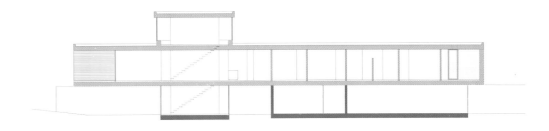

Left: Exterior. Links: Außenansicht. À gauche: Façade principale. | Right: Longitudinal section. Rechts: Längsschnitt. À droite: Coupe longitudinale.

The single-family home, located on a slope, consists of a 45-meter narrow wooden structure, placed on a small number of steel supports along the contour line, as well as a concrete support wall above the property. With a recessed balcony positioned in front, all façades offer a view of Lake Constance and are glazed floor to ceiling, seamlessly connecting the interior to the exterior. The wide eaves of the recessed balcony protect the building from overheating, while enabling the sun to enter in the winter. For ecologic reasons, only untreated materials were used for the low-energy house.

Das Einfamilienhaus, an einem Hang gelegen, besteht aus einem 45 Meter langen schmalen Baukörper aus Holz und ist entlang der Höhenlinie auf einigen wenigen Stahlstützen sowie einer Betonstützmauer über dem Grundstück angelegt. Sämtliche Fassaden mit Blick auf den Bodensee sind mit vorgelagerter Loggia raumhoch verglast und verbinden übergangslos den Innenraum mit dem Außenraum. Die weiten Dachvorsprünge der Loggia schützen im Sommer vor zu großer Erhitzung des Gebäudes und erlauben im Winter eine angenehme Sonneneinstrahlung. Aus ökologischen Gründen sind alle verwendeten Materialien des als Niedrigenergiehauses konzipierten Wohnhauses naturbelassen.

Cette maison individuelle de quarante-cinq mètres de long a été construite sur un terrain en pente. Elle se compose d'un étage en bois posé sur des piliers et un socle en béton. Les deux façades qui donnent sur le lac de Constance sont entièrement vitrées de manière à assurer un lien progressif entre l'intérieur et l'extérieur. La véranda et le toit en surplomb assurent une bonne régulation thermique été comme hiver. Ce bâtiment répond à un concept résolument écologique puisque aucun des matériaux n'a été traité, tandis que la consommation énergétique a été réduite au minimum.

From left to right, from above to below:
Interior with deck, deck, exterior from below.
Right: Fireplace and dining area.

Von links nach rechts, von oben nach unten:
Innenasicht mit Terrasse, Aussicht vom Wohnzimmer, Talansicht.
Rechts: Küche mit Kamin.

De gauche à droite, du haut vers le bas:
Deux vues de l'intérieur et de la terrasse, vue d'ensemble.
À droite: Salle à manger avec cheminée.

ARCHITEKTUR.TERMINAL HACKL UND KLAMMER

www.architekturterminal.at
Client: Gabriele und Günter Tschütscher, **Completion:** 2008, **Gross floor area:** 214 m², **Photos:** Roswitha Natter.

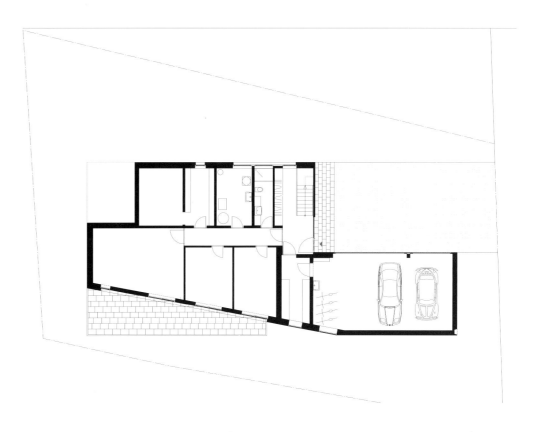

Left: Exterior with deck. Links: Außenansicht mit Terrasse. À gauche: Vue de la terrasse. | Right: Floor plan. Rechts: Grundriss. À droite: Plan.

The slight northern slope offers a panoramic view of the Walgau and the mountainous Rätikon region. The plot is shaped like a parallelogram, with the slope extending diagonally across it. The shape of the house is derived from the topography and defines the driveway with the front courtyard. The flexed façade reacts to the various height lines and the borders of the plot, while the roof corresponds to the angle of the slope. The entrance area and a sheltered balcony are integrated into the structure. To the south, the living room opens up towards the connected terrace landscape with a roofed seating area and immediate ground-floor access to the natural environment.

Der leichte Nordhang bietet einen Panoramablick über den Walgau und die Bergwelt des Rätikons. Das Grundstück hat die Form eines Parallelogramms, die Hangneigung verläuft diagonal über die Grundstücksform. Die Form des Hauses leitet sich aus der Topografie ab und definiert die Zufahrt mit Vorplatz. Die geknickte Fassade reagiert auf die Höhenschichtenlinien und den Grundgrenzenverlauf, das Dach entspricht der Hangneigung. Der Eingangsbereich und ein geschützter Balkon sind im Baukörper integriert. Südseitig öffnet sich der Wohnraum auf die vorgelagerte Terrassenlandschaft mit überdachtem Sitzplatz und direktem, ebenerdigem Zugang in die Naturlandschaft.

Cette maison construite sur un versant nord en pente douce offre un panorama sur le Walgau et le massif du Raetikon. Le terrain en forme de parallélogramme et la topographie des lieux ont déterminé l'aspect du bâtiment et de l'esplanade d'entrée. Avec pour résultat une façade en ligne brisée, un toit dont l'inclinaison correspond à la pente du terrain et un balcon abrité intégré à l'ensemble. Du côté sud, le séjour donne sur une terrasse partiellement protégée par un surplomb du toit d'où l'on accède directement à la nature environnante.

From left to right, from above to below:
Exterior, living room, bathroom.
Right: Living room with view of dining room.

Von links nach rechts, von oben nach unten:
Außenansicht, Wohnzmmer, Badezimmer.
Rechts: Wohnzimmer mit Kamin.

De gauche à droite, du haut vers le bas:
Extérieur, séjour, salle de bain.
À droite:: Séjour avec cheminée.

HOUSE PFITZ,

LINZ, AUSTRIA

ARCHITEKT DI MATTHIAS LANGMAYR

Client: Dr. Georg & Christina Langmayr, Completion: 2003, Gross floor area: 192 m², Photos: Christoph Goldmann.

Left: Exterior view with pool. Links: Außenansicht mit Swimmingpool. À gauche: Villa et piscine. | Right: First floor plan. Rechts: Grundriss Erdgeschoss. À droite: Plan du rez-de-chaussée.

The characteristics of the residence are not immediately apparent to visitors. The building attempts to create a spatial tension through its vertical alignment. The roof floor accommodates two terraces and features large-scale glazing. This glass façade offers an panoramic view of the entire Mühlviertel district. Larch wood was used for the paneling of the façade, extending across the roof area as well.

Das Wohnhaus offenbart sich dem Besucher nicht auf den ersten Blick. Mit einer vertikalen Ausrichtung versucht das Gebäude, eine räumliche Spannung aufzubauen. Das Dachgeschoss bietet Platz für zwei Terrassen und ist großflächig verglast. Diese Glasfassade ermöglicht einen Panoramablick über das gesamte Mühlviertel. Für die Verschalung der Fassade wurde Lärchenholz verwendet, das sich bis über die Dachfläche zieht.

Les qualités de cette villa se révèlent lors d'une étude approfondie. La verticalité du bâtiment crée une certaine tension spatiale. Le dernier étage dispose de deux terrasses et de murs entièrement vitrés qui offrent des vues panoramiques sur les environs. Toutes les façades et même le toit sont entièrement bardées de planches de mélèze.

From left to right, from above to below:
Sundeck view, street side view, living space, hallway.
Right: Rear view.

Von links nach rechts, von oben nach unten:
Terrassenansicht, Straßenansicht, Wohnraum, Flur.
Rechts: Rückansicht.

De gauche à droite, du haut vers le bas:
Terrasse, villa vue de la route, séjour, couloir.
À droite: Face arrière.

EFH_LUDESCH,
LUDESCH, AUSTRIA

K_M.ARCHITEKTUR DI DANIEL SAUTER

www.k-m-architektur.com

Client: Private, **Completion:** 2008, **Gross floor area:** 150 m², **Photos:** Courtesy of k_m.architektur DI Daniel Sauter.

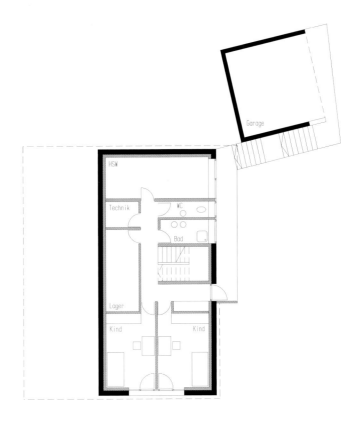

Left: Side view. Links: Seitenansicht. À gauche: Vue latérale. | Right: Ground floor plan. Rechts: Grundriss. À droite: Plan du rez-de-chaussée.

The two-floor residential home was built on a strongly sloping plot with a plateau. The mountain panorama is already visible for visitors from the stairway located in the north of the structure through the open living and dining area. On the upper floor, the open kitchen is located next to this area, along with the bedroom facing east, the bathroom, and an office. The façade of the wooden upper floor is made of horizontal white fir planes. Untreated white fir wood was also used for the floors, ceilings and windows. The ground floor contains functional rooms and the children's bedrooms with access to the garden.

Das zweigeschossige Wohnhaus wurde auf einem stark abschüssigen Grundstück mit Plateau errichtet. Das Bergpanorama erschließt sich dem Besucher bereits vom im Norden des Baukörpers gelegenen Treppenhauses durch den offen gestalteten Wohn- und Essbereich. Im Obergeschoss finden sich neben diesem Bereich die offene Küche und der nach Osten orientierte Schlafraum, das Bad und ein Büro. Die Fassade des aus Holzrahmenbauweise bestehenden Obergeschosses ist aus horizontaler Weißtannenverschalung. Dieses unbehandelte Holz wurde ebenfalls für die Fußböden, Decken und Fenster verwendet.

Cette maison sur deux niveaux a été construite sur un terrain partiellement en pente raide. L'entrée et l'escalier se trouvent au nord et l'on aperçoit un magnifique panorama de montagnes dès qu'on accède au salon/salle à manger entièrement vitré. C'est également à ce niveau que se trouvent la cuisine ouverte, la chambre, la salle de bain et le bureau. Cet étage est pourvu d'un bardage en planches de sapin blanc non traitées disposées horizontalement. Le même matériau a été utilisé pour le parquet, le plafond et les fenêtres. Au niveau inférieur se trouvent divers locaux techniques ainsi que les chambres des enfants qui disposent d'un accès direct au jardin.

From left to right, from above to below:
Interior with fireplace, deck, dining area.
Right: Exterior with deck.

Von links nach rechts, von oben nach unten:
Wohnraum mit Kamin, Terrasse, offene Küche.
Rechts: Außenansicht mit Terrasse.

De gauche à droite, du haut vers le bas:
Intérieur, terrasse, salle à manger.
À droite: Vue côté jardin.

HOUSE MÜHLGRABEN,
MÜHLGRABEN, AUSTRIA

MAAARS ARCHITECTURE

www.maaars.com

Client: Helene & Clemens Schnitzer-Bruch, **Completion:** 2007, **Gross floor area:** 115 m², **Photos:** Bruno Klomfar.

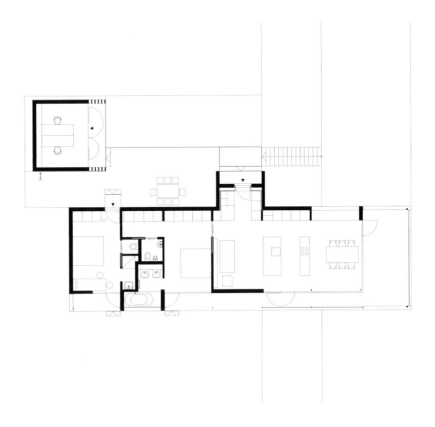

Left: Exterior by night. Links: Außenansicht bei Nacht. À gauche: L'extérieur la nuit. | Right: Floor plan. Rechts: Grundriss. À droite: Plan.

The long main body of the dwelling incorporates standard features for cooking, living, and sleeping, as well as a guestroom and accompanying bathroom facilities. A one-storied pre-fabricated structure made out of solid timber lamella was built onto a south-facing cantilevered concrete base. The intention was to achieve a smooth transition between the interior and exterior space. Specific building materials were chosen to align with the concept of renewable energy. Nano-technology was used on the outer casing of the house to prevent weathering.

Das längliche, gestreckte Haupthaus beherbergt die Standardfunktionen Kochen, Wohnen, Schlafen, ein Gästezimmer und die dazugehörigen Nasszellen. Auf einer südseitig auskragenden Betonbasis wurde eine eingeschossige Fertigteilkonstruktion aus Massivholzlamellen aufgesetzt. Der Übergang zwischen Innen- und Außenraum sollte fließend sein und die Natur in das Hausinnere transferiert werden. Die Auswahl der Baustoffe hatte dem Energiekonzept, welches ausschließlich auf erneuerbare Energieträger ausgerichtet werden sollte, zu entsprechen. Die komplette Außenhülle wurde mittels Nano-Technologie vor Verwitterung geschützt.

Dans cette maison toute en longueur, on trouve une cuisine, un séjour, des chambres et des salles d'eau. Une base en béton supporte un étage en lamelles de bois préfabriquées en porte-à-faux du côté sud. Le passage de l'extérieur à l'intérieur se fait de manière fluide afin de mieux intégrer la nature aux espaces habitables. Les matériaux de construction ont été strictement sélectionnés en fonction de leur compatibilité avec les énergies renouvelables. Afin de maximiser la protection face aux intempéries, tout le revêtement de façade a bénéficié d'un traitement utilisant les nanotechnologies.

From left to right, from above to below:
Rear view, kitchen and dining area, wrap around terrace.
Right: Glazed façade by night.

Von links nach rechts, von oben nach unten:
Rückansicht, Küche und Essecke, umlaufende Terrasse.
Rechts: Verglaste Fassade bei Nacht.

De gauche à droite, du haut vers le bas:
Face arrière, cuisine et salle à manger, terrasse.
À droite: Façade la nuit.

HOUSE WUCHER,
RAGGAL, AUSTRIA

MAAARS ARCHITECTURE

www.maaars.com
Client: Christian Wucher, **Completion:** 2007, **Gross floor area:** 90 m², **Photos:** Bruno Klomfar.

Left: Exterior by night. Links: Außenansicht bei Nacht. À gauche: L'extérieur la nuit. | Right: Floor plans. Rechts: Grundrisse. À droite: Plans.

In order to merge into the landscape naturally, the residence, which is inhabited all year round, intentionally avoids typical urban exterior characteristics. The use of untreated wood paneling on the front face of the building and the shingled roof reinforce this impression of rusticity. This stands in contrast to other intricate elements of the house, such as the inclined row of windows, viewing slots, corner windows and solar energy plants. By incorporating traditional and modern features whilst also taking the surrounding countryside into consideration, this timber structure attempts to be an instrument of historical continuity.

Das ganzjährig bewohnte Haus verzichtet auf urbane Elemente und Ausdrucksformen – insbesondere in der Außenraum- und Umgebungsgestaltung, sodass der Hauskörper selbstverständlich im Landschaftsraum liegt. Die von rohen Viertelrundhölzern filterartig verkleideten Stirnseiten verstärken mit dem Schindeldach die Rustikalität des Eindrucks. Dieser wird jedoch klug kontrastiert von liegenden Fensterbändern, Sichtschlitzen, Eckverglasungen, und Solarkollektoren. Der Holzbau wird hier zum Vehikel historischer Kontinuität: respektvoll gegenüber der (Haus-)Landschaft, der Vergangenheit und Gegenwart.

Ce chalet habité en permanence rejette tout élément typiquement urbain. C'est particulièrement vrai dans les espaces extérieurs, l'édifice apparaissant comme planté dans le paysage. Le toit en shingles et les quarts-de-rond en bois brut qui servent de filtres solaires sur les pignons renforcent encore la rusticité de l'ensemble. Celle-ci forme un contraste intelligent avec divers éléments modernes tels que les bandes de fenêtres horizontales, les angles vitrés et les capteurs solaires. Cette construction majoritairement en bois s'inscrit ainsi dans la continuité historique en respectant à la fois le paysage, le passé et le présent.

From left to right, from above to below:
Living / dining room, panoramic window, kitchen / dining room.
Right: Exterior view.

Von links nach rechts, von oben nach unten:
Wohn- und Esszimmer, Panoramablick, Küche mit Essecke.
Rechts: Außenansicht.

De gauche à droite, du haut vers le bas:
Salle de séjour / salle à manger, fenêtre panoramique,
cuisine /salle à manger.
À droite: Extérieur.

HOUSE WITHIN A HOUSE,
SCHLINS, AUSTRIA

ARCHITEKTUR.TERMINAL HACKL
UND KLAMMER

www.architekturterminal.at

Client: Madlener family, **Completion:** 2003, **Gross floor area:** 390 m², **Photos:** Courtesy of architektur.
terminal hackl und klammer.

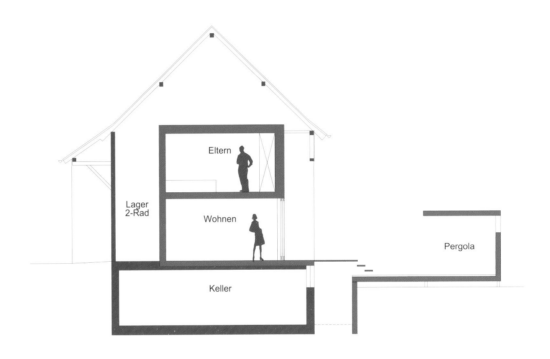

Left: Exterior with covered parking. Links: Außenansicht mit Carport. À gauche: Maison et garage ouvert. | Right: Section. Rechts: Schnitt.
À droite: Vue en coupe.

The available space of the small farmhouse was extended by an additional construction, resulting in a "house within a house". The number of new openings was limited so as not to disrupt the character of the existing building, while deliberately applying the context of old and new. The dark wooden panels were maintained as a hull. The open gaps of the cover offer interesting views, creating a dialog between the exterior and interior. The living room located upstairs is reached via a bridge and is positioned above the new bedroom.

Die Vergrößerung des Raumangebots im Kleinbauernhaus wurde mit Hilfe eines eingebauten Volumens realisiert. So entstand die Konstruktion „Haus im Haus". Um den Charakter des bestehenden Objektes nicht zu stören, wurde die Zahl der neuen Öffnungen gering gehalten, jedoch bewusst im Kontext von Alt und Neu gesetzt, dabei ist die dunkle Holzverschalung als Ummantelung erhalten geblieben. Die offenen Fugen der Verkleidung bieten interessante Ein- und Ausblicke und bilden einen Dialog zwischen Innen und Außen. Das im Obergeschoss gelegene Schlafzimmer wird über eine Brücke erreicht und befindet sich über dem neuen Wohnzimmer.

Afin d'augmenter la surface habitable dans une ancienne ferme de dimensions réduites, les architectes ont appliqué le concept de « maison dans la maison » qui permet de préserver l'aspect général des bâtiments d'origine. Ils ont ainsi aménagé la grange en conservant le revêtement en planches patinées et en perçant un nombre minimum d'ouvertures. Les interstices entre les vieilles planches intensifient le dialogue entre l'intérieur et l'extérieur. Une passerelle permet d'accéder à la chambre située au premier étage, au-dessus du nouveau séjour.

GÉOMÉTRIE BLEUE,
ÎLES DE LA MADELEINE, QC, CANADA

YH2

www.yh2architecture.com

Client: Private, **Completion:** 2004, **Gross floor area:** 165 m², **Photos:** Jeff Mcnamara (54), Loukas Yiacouvakis (56 a.), Philippe Saharoff.

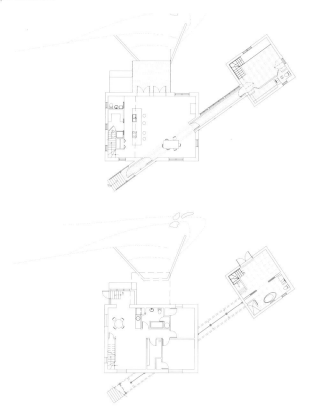

Left: Exterior view of sister houses. Links: Außenansicht. À gauche: Vue des maisons-sœurs. | Right: Floor plans. Rechts: Grundrisse. À droite: Plans.

The idea of this project was to expand and transform an existing house to create a true holiday home for the owners and their guests in the spirit of typical Magdalen Island structures. Instead of expanding the existing structure, a second, distinct, autonomous building, the private domain of the owners, was constructed and joined to the present building by a closed overhead cedar walkway. The existing house was transformed into a common area and the new building reserved for the owners. The result: two sister houses in chalk-like blue, an attempt to capture a childhood drawing, the outside in cedar shingles, and the all-white inside boarded in pine.

Ein Wohnhaus sollte erweitert und in ein Feriendomizil umgewandelt werden. Dabei musste sich das Projekt am Charakter der typischen Bauten auf Magdalen Island orientieren. Anstatt das vorhandene Gebäude zu ergänzen, wurde eine zweite eigenständige Konstruktion errichtet und durch einen geschlossenen, hoch liegenden Fußweg aus Zedernholz mit dem Bestand verbunden. Das vorhandene Haus wurde für die gemeinschaftliche Nutzung mit Gästen umgebaut, der Neubau dem Privatbereich der Eigentümer vorbehalten. Die beiden kreidestiftähnlichen Bauten sollen an eine Kinderzeichnung erinnern. Außen sind sie mit Zedernholz eingeschindelt und in dem ganz weiß gehaltenen Innern mit Kiefernholz verkleidet.

L'objectif était ici d'agrandir et de transformer un édifice préexistant pour en faire une maison de vacances dans le style traditionnel des îles de la Madeleine. Au lieu de construire directement à partir du bâtiment d'origine, les architectes ont ajouté un édifice autonome, les deux volumes étant reliés par un passage couvert avec bardeaux en cèdre. Avec pour résultat final des maisons-sœurs à l'intérieur blanc et aux façades bleues peintes à la chaux — images d'une maison issue de l'enfance dessinée à la craie.

From left to right, from above to below:
Exterior, living room and kitchen, hallway.
Right: Bathroom.

Von links nach rechts, von oben nach unten:
Verbindungsbau, offene Küche und Wohnbreich, Flur.
Rechts: Badezimmer.

De gauche à droite, du haut vers le bas:
Extérieur, chambre, couloir.
À droite: Salle de bain.

MOLLY'S CABIN,
POINTE AU BARIL, ON, CANADA

AGATHOM CO.

www.agathom.com
Client: Molly Thom, **Completion:** 2008, **Gross floor area:** 88 m², **Photos:** Paul Orenstein.

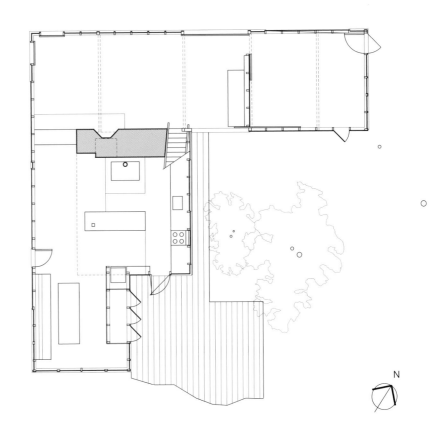

Left: Interior with fireplace. Links: Wohnzimmer mit Kamin. À gauche: Intérieur avec cheminée centrale. | **Right:** Floor plan. Rechts: Grundriss. À droite: Plan.

Located in Georgian Bay on a cusp of the Canadian Shield, this private seasonal retreat aims to balance comfort with the bare necessities so that its inhabitants live lightly on the land and fully engage with their surroundings. The cabin fits snugly against the boulders and is sited close to the edge of the water. Shielded behind a large rock and a signature tree, there are multiple views of the fast-changing weather from under the shelter of the tent-like flaps. Topped by a broad shingled asphalt roof and constructed from recovered timbers, the cabin is anchored by a Rumford fireplace that makes use of local stone.

In der Georgian Bay auf einer Spitze des Kanadischen Schilds gelegen, soll dieses private, saisonal nutzbare Refugium eine Balance zwischen Komfort und Grundbedürfnissen halten, damit seine Bewohner in einem direkten Dialog mit ihrer Umgebung stehen. Die den Felsblöcken genau eingepasste Holzkonstruktion steht nahe dem Ufer. Hinter einem großen Stein und einem Baum verborgen, bietet sie unter den zeltähnlichen Klappen vielfältige Aussichten auf das sich schnell verändernde Wetter. Das aus Altholz errichtete Haus wird von einem Asphaltdach mit breiten Schindeln bedeckt und von einem Rumford-Kamin aus lokalem Stein charakterisiert.

Cette maison de vacances construite à Georgian Bay, sur le bouclier canadien, réalise un compromis entre le confort et le minimum nécessaire, afin de privilégier le contact direct des occupants avec la nature environnante. Le bâtiment est posé directement sur la roche, à proximité immédiate de l'eau. Protégé par un grand rocher et un arbre typique de la région, il permet d'apprécier la nature tout en bénéficiant d'un abri face aux vicissitudes du temps, particulièrement changeant ici. La maison se caractérise principalement par un grand toit en shingles goudronnés, des murs en bois recyclé et une grande cheminée de type Rumford en pierres d'origine locale.

Exterior with landscape view. Gesamtansicht. Maison construite sur la roche.

From left to right, from above to below:
Deck, interior, entrance.
Right: Kitchen.

Von links nach rechts, von oben nach unten:
Terrasse, Wohnzimmer mit Aussicht, Eingangsbereich.
Rechts: Offene Küche.

De gauche à droite, du haut vers le bas:
Terrasse, intérieur, entrée.
À droite: Cuisine ouverte.

MOUNTAIN REFUGE LOS CANTEROS,

FARELLONES, LOS CONDES, CHILE

DRN ARCHITECTS
IN COLLABORATION WITH
OLTMANN AHLERS

www.drn.cl

Client: Moral family, **Completion:** 2008, **Gross floor area:** 140 m², **Photos:** Felipe Camus.

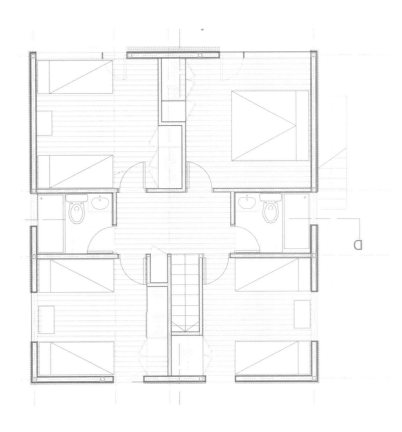

Left: Exterior with deck and stairs. Links: Außenansicht. À gauche: Vue latérale avec terrasse et escaliers. | Right: Floor plan. Rechts: Grundriss. À droite: Plan.

The site was an existing void in the middle of a slope, bound on two sides by magnificent old containment walls built of stone. This contemporary mountain refuge uses a monolithic volume of stone that partially fills the void left by the walls. Window openings are minimal and were placed so as to illuminate specific acts, or to frame certain parts of the surrounding landscape, keeping away the sight of the neighbors. This simple stone cube is broken up by other elements that overhang from its perimeter, modifying the basic figure and giving it an orientation towards specific external features.

Das Grundstück, eine Lücke in der Mitte eines Hangs, war an zwei Seiten von prächtigen alten Begrenzungsmauern aus Naturstein flankiert. Diese moderne Berghütte füllt den Raum zwischen den Mauern mit einem monolithischen steinernen Baukörper teilweise aus. Ein Minimum an Fenstern akzentuiert besondere Funktionen oder rahmt bestimmte Teile der umliegenden Landschaft ein, wobei Nachbarblicke ferngehalten werden. Der einfache Steinkubus wird von anderen Bauteilen aufgelöst, die über seine Außenränder hervorkragen. Sie verändern die Ausgangsform und richten sie zu spezifischen äußeren Merkmalen aus.

Ce refuge a été construit à flanc de montagne entre deux anciens murets de soutènement en pierres naturelles. Il s'agit d'un bâtiment monolithique qui remplit partiellement l'espace compris entre les murets. Les ouvertures, de taille minimale, sont disposées de manière à éclairer certains espaces intérieurs et à offrir des vues sur le paysage environnant, tout en laissant l'intérieur à l'abri des regards indiscrets. Le volume cubique à parement de pierre s'enrichit d'éléments en porte-à-faux aux endroits présentant un intérêt particulier.

Left: Exterior at sunset. Links: Außenansicht. Gauche: Le chalet au crépuscule. **Right**: Deck view. **Rechts**: Terrasse. À droite: Terrasse.

From left to right, from above to below:
Façade detail, exterior view across a field of snow, interior.
Right: Exterior at night.

Von links nach rechts, von oben nach unten:
Fassade, Talansicht, Wohnbereich mit Aussicht.
Rechts: Außenansicht bei Nacht.

De gauche à droite, du haut vers le bas:
Détail de la façade, le chalet vu d'un champ de neige
en contrebas, intérieur.
À droite: Le chalet la nuit.

CHALET C6,
LOS ANDES, CHILE

DRN ARCHITECTS

www.drn.cl
Client: Hotel Portillo, Completion: 2006, Gross floor area: 240 m², Photos: Max Núñez.

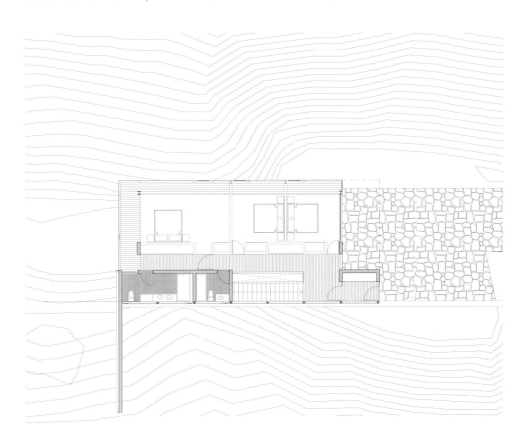

Left: Exterior with lake view. Links: Außenansicht mit Blick auf den See. À gauche: Chalet près du lac. | Right: Floor plan. Rechts: Grundriss. À droite: Plan.

This ski chalet for two avid skiers had to disappear from the view of the Hotel behind it during the winter months. The architects were able to take full advantage of the sweeping vistas to the Inca Lagoon and the Tres Hermanos mountains to the north, while still working within the design constraints of six-meter deep snow and ice loads. The result is an amazing structure that manages to retain inner warmth despite the freezing temperatures outside. This silent architecture integrates extreme weather, open landscape and comfort and snow as a finishing material.

Diese Skihütte für zwei begeisterte Skifahrer sollte in den Wintermonaten von dem hinter ihr liegenden Hotel aus nicht zu sehen sein. Den Architekten gelang es, die überwältigenden Aussichten auf die Inca-Lagune und die Berge Tres Hermanos im Norden gänzlich ausnutzen, obwohl die Konstruktion sechs Meter hohem Schnee und Eislasten standhalten muss. Der verblüffende Bau bewahrt trotz der eisigen Außentemperaturen eine behagliche Innenatmosphäre. Seine zurückhaltende Architektur kombiniert eine extreme Witterung, eine offene Landschaft, Komfort und Schnee.

En hiver, ce chalet construit dans une station de ski est pratiquement invisible de l'hôtel qui se trouve à proximité. Les architectes ont parfaitement su l'intégrer au site magnifique du lac de l'Inca, dominé par le triple sommet des Tres Hermanos, tout en tenant compte des contraintes imposées par la glace et une épaisseur de neige pouvant aller jusqu'à six mètres. Leur réalisation d' « architecture silencieuse » est remarquable par sa bonne adaptation aux températures extrêmes qui règnent ici, et par le confort qu'elle garantit tout en ménageant des vues sur le paysage environnant et la neige omniprésente.

From left to right, from above to below:
Interior, exterior, lake view.
Right: Exterior.

Von links nach rechts, von oben nach unten:
Wonbereicht mit Blick auf den See, Außenansicht, Seeblick.
Rechts: Talansicht.

De gauche à droite, du haut vers le bas:
Intérieur, extérieur, vue du lac.
À droite: Chalet vu d'en bas avec l'hôtel à l'arrière plan.

CHALET C7,
LOS ANDES, CHILE

DRN ARCHITECTS

www.drn.cl

Client: Hotel Portillo, **Completion:** 2008, **Gross floor area:** 240 m², **Photos:** Max Núñez, Felipe Camus.

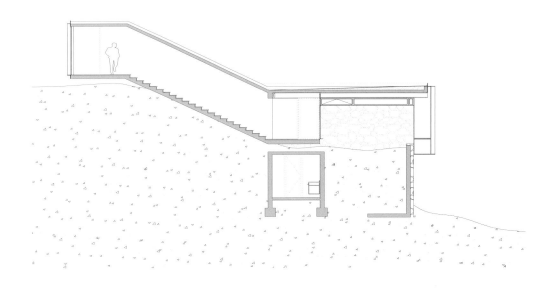

Left: Stone façade. Links: Steinfassade. À gauche: Chalet au bord du lac. | **Right:** Section. Rechts: Schnitt. À droite: Vue en coupe.

The project is located at 2,990 meters above sea level in the Andes Mountains. The site is on the south slope of the Inca Lake, just in front of the Portillo Hotel, a few kilometers away of the Argentinean border and Mount Aconcagua. The terrain is a steep rocky slope, facing the immediate view to the lake and the Tres Hermanos Mountains. Over this strong and harsh natural landscape the house disappears from its view uphill, without interfering the view towards the lake. From a protected environment, inside the refuge, the mountain landscape is the main character.

Das Projekt liegt in den Anden auf einer Höhe von 2.990 Meter über dem Meeresspiegel. Sein Grundstück befindet sich am Südhang des Sees Inca direkt gegenüber dem Hotel Portillo, wenige Kilometer von der argentinischen Grenze und dem Berg Aconcagua entfernt. Von diesem steilen Felshang geht der Blick unmittelbar auf den See und die Berge Tres Hermanos. In der schroffen, natürlichen Landschaft ist das Haus bei einer bergauf gerichteten Betrachtung kaum wahrnehmbar und verstellt nicht die Sicht auf den See. Von der geschützten Umgebung des Refugiums aus dominiert die Berglandschaft.

Ce chalet est situé dans les Andes à 2990 mètres d'altitude, sur la rive sud du lac de l'Inca, c'est-à-dire à quelques kilomètres seulement de l'Aconcagua et de la frontière avec l'Argentine. Il est construit sur un terrain en pente, près d'un hôtel avec vue sur le triple sommet des Tres Hermanos. Le bâtiment s'intègre parfaitement au site grandiose et rude, sans gêner le panorama sur le lac à partir de l'hôtel voisin. Les architectes ont fait un usage abondant des panneaux vitrés de manière à ouvrir largement le chalet sur la montagne toute proche.

Left: Living area with fireplace. Links: Wohnbereich mit Kamin. À gauche: Séjour avec cheminée. **Right:** Lakeside view. Rechts: Dachansicht. À droite: Vue plongeante sur le toit du chalet et le lac.

From left to right, from above to below:
Exterior, alternative view of exterior, living area.
Right: Bedroom with panoramic view.

Von links nach rechts, von oben nach unten:
Ansicht, Terrasse, Wohnzimmer mit Kamin.
Rechts: Schlafzimmer mit Seeblick.

De gauche à droite, du haut vers le bas:
Deux vues de l'extérieur, séjour.
À droite: Chambre avec vue sur le lac.

METAMORPHOSIS OF A WOODEN HOUSE,
TUNQUÉN, CASABLANCA, CHILE

JOSÉ ULLOA DAVET + DELPHINE DING

www.delphineding.com
Client: Elena Davet Pavlov, **Completion:** 2008, **Gross floor area:** 180 m², **Photos:** Courtesy of José Ulloa Davet + Delphine Ding.

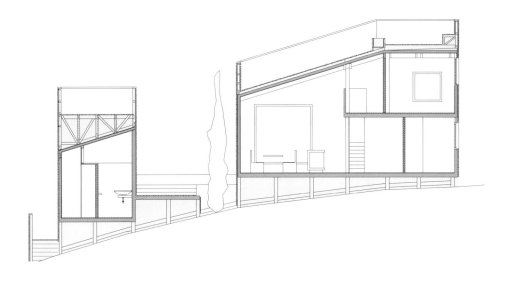

Left: Exterior with landscaped yard. Links: Holzfassade. À gauche: Vue d'ensemble. | Right: Section. Rechts: Schnitt. À droite: Vue en coupe.

This project is conceived as the metamorphosis of a wooden house, creating a new shape with stronger bond to the landscape. What used to be the roof of the house is transformed into a panoramic deck, which allows public access. A new room is cantilevered over the entrance, generating an access porch, which protects the space below from the sun and rain. The new areas of the house are blended with the existing through the ventilated timber skin, which brings greater durability and thermal stability to the façade by protecting it from the weather conditions. Its design is structured in a three-four rhythm, a texture that is only interrupted by the square-shaped openings that frame the landscape.

Das als Metamorphose eines Holzhauses konzipierte Projekt schafft eine neue Form mit einem stärkeren Bezug zur Landschaft. Aus dem ursprünglichen Dach des Hauses wird ein öffentlich zugängliches Panoramadeck. Über dem Eingang kragt ein neuer, überdachter Raum hervor, der vor Sonne und Regen schützt. Eine hinterlüftete Außenbeplankung lässt die neuen Bereiche des Hauses mit dem Bestand verschmelzen. Als Witterungsschutz erhöht sie die Haltbarkeit der Fassade und dämmt sie. Ihre Gestaltung in einem Dreiviertelrhythmus ergibt eine Textur, die nur von den rechteckigen Fenstern unterbrochen wird, welche die Landschaft rahmen.

Une ancienne maison en bois s'est métamorphosée pour mieux intégrer le paysage. Le toit est devenu une terrasse panoramique, tandis qu'une pièce supplémentaire était rajoutée au-dessus de l'entrée, le surplomb formant une sorte de porche qui protège à la fois du soleil et de la pluie. Une enveloppe ventilée en bois unifie l'ancien et le nouveau, tout en assurant à long terme une bonne isolation thermique de l'intérieur. Ce revêtement aux trois quarts s'ouvre par des fenêtres carrées qui offrent des vues magnifiques sur le paysage environnant.

Exterior with deck. Terrasse mit Aufgang zur Dachterrasse. Vue d'ensemble.

From left to right, from above to below:
Façade detail, living room, exterior, façade detail.
Right: Deck with ocean view.

Von links nach rechts, von oben nach unten:
Detailansicht, Blick ins Wohnzimmer,
Gesamtansicht, Fensterdetail.
Rechts: Plattform mit Ozeanansicht.

De gauche à droite, du haut vers le bas:
Détail de la façade, séjour, deux autres vues de l'extérieur.
À droite: Terrasse avec vue sur l'océan.

HIP CHALETS / JAMIE STRACHAN
(INTERIOR DESIGN)
DYNAMIC HIP

www.le-marti.com
Client: Dynamic Hip, **Completion:** 2007, **Gross floor area:** 350 m², **Photos:** Jeremy Wilson.

Left: Bedroom. Links: Schlafzimmer. À gauche: Chambre. | Right: Floor plans. Rechts: Grundrisse. À droite: Plans.

This boutique hotel-styled chalet was once the village school in the old village of Argentiere at the foot of Mont Blanc. It later became a hostel for walkers and climbers and it was also for a while a restaurant. Today Le Marti is a modernized chalet designed by Hip Chalets, blending contemporary design with rustic features. The 340 square meter of living area holds a sauna and outdoor hot tub, eight bedrooms with ensuite bathrooms, an open plan lounge and dining area separated by a modern fireplace. Le Marti is the perfect modern getaway for ski lovers as its location is right below the world famous ski area Les Grands Montets in the heart of the Mont Blanc valley.

Das Chalet im Stil eines Boutique-Hotels ist die ehemalige Dorfschule in Argentière am Fuße des Mont Blancs. Später diente sie als Herberge für Wanderer und Bergsteiger und eine Zeit lang auch als Restaurant. Heute vermischt sich in dem von Hip Chalets entworfenen, modernisierten Bau ein zeitgemäßes Design mit rustikalen Merkmalen. Auf 340 Quadratmetern enthält es eine Sauna und einen Außenwhirlpool, acht Zimmer mit eigenem Bad sowie einen offenen, von einem modernen Kamin abgetrennten Aufenthalts- und Essbereich. Le Marti ist der ideale Ort für Skifreunde, da es direkt unterhalb des weltberühmten Skigebiets Les Grands Montets mitten im Tal des Mont Blancs liegt.

Ce chalet a été aménagé dans l'ancienne école d'Argentière, village savoyard typique niché au pied du mont Blanc. C'était auparavant un restaurant et un gîte pour randonneurs et alpinistes. Modernisé par Hip Chalets, c'est aujourd'hui une résidence haut de gamme qui associe la tradition rustique et le design contemporain. Sur une surface habitable de 340 mètres carrés, le chalet abrite un sauna, une baignoire en plein air, huit chambres avec salle de bain ainsi qu'un salon à plan ouvert avec cheminée et espace salle à manger. L'endroit est très apprécié des skieurs du fait de sa position au pied des pistes des Grands Montets.

From left to right, from above to below:
Bathroom, double bedroom, dining room, Jacuzzi.
Right: Living room with fireplace.

Von links nach rechts, von oben nach unten:
Badezimmer, Doppelzimmer, Esszimmer, Whirlpool.
Rechts: Wohnzimmer mit Kamin.

De gauche à droite, du haut vers le bas:
Salle de bain, chambre double, salle à manger, jacuzzi.
À droite: Séjour avec cheminée.

CHALET DES DRUS,

CHAMONIX, FRANCE

FMP LEFÈVRE

www.hipchalets.com

Client: Philippe Dapsens, **Completion:** 2009, **Gross floor area:** 600 m², **Photos:** Erlend Haugen.

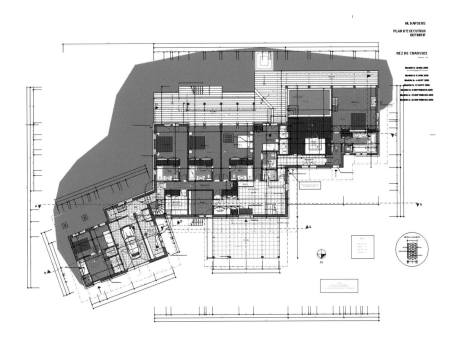

Left: Bedroom with fireplace. Links: Schlafzimmer mit Kamin. À gauche: Chambre à coucher avec cheminée. | Right: Ground floor plan. Rechts: Grundriss Erdgeschoss. À droite: Plan du rez-de-chaussée.

Le Chalet des Drus has bespoke furnishings designed exclusively for the chalet and original works of art from the owner's personal collection. The chalets' façade and interiors combine burned and sand blasted rustic wood, beautiful stonework and stucco plaster work on some interior walls. The use of these traditional materials contrasts beautifully with the modern design features such as the glass stairway and slate dining table using iron legs from the workshop of Mr. Eiffel, (architect of the Eiffel Tower). This creates a stunning harmony respecting traditional building materials, and techniques with modern design features and technology.

Dieses Chalet ist mit maßgefertigten Möbeln und Originalkunstwerken aus der Privatsammlung des Eigentümers ausgestattet. An der Fassade und im Inneren finden sich verkohltes und gesandeltes rustikales Holz, Natursteinmauerwerk sowie Gipsputzarbeiten an einigen Innenwänden. Diese traditionellen Materialien bilden einen attraktiven Kontrast mit den modernen Gestaltungsmerkmalen wie der Glastreppe und dem Esstisch aus Schiefer mit eisernen Beinen aus der Werkstatt des Erbauers des Eiffelturms. Dadurch entsteht eine inspirierende Harmonie, die traditionellen Baumaterialien ebenso Rechnung trägt wie einem zeitgemäßen Design und moderner Technik.

La décoration intérieure de ce chalet intègre des murs en stuc, des meubles faits sur mesure et des œuvres d'art originales issues de la collection personnelle du propriétaire. La pierre et le bois brut sont omniprésents, tant à l'intérieur qu'à l'extérieur. Ces matériaux traditionnels s'inscrivent en contraste par rapport à des éléments de style design, notamment la cage d'escalier en verre et la table de la salle à manger, composée d'un plateau en ardoise reposant des pieds en fer fabriqués dans les ateliers de Gustave Eiffel. Cette alliance de la tradition savoyarde et de la technologie moderne est stupéfiante d'harmonie.

From left to right, from above to below:
Fireplace, dining and lounge area, bathroom, interior detail.
Right: Exterior with view to mountains.

Von links nach rechts, von oben nach unten:
Kamin, Speise- und Aufenthaltsraum, Badezimmer, Innenraumdetail.
Rechts: Außenansicht mit Blick auf die Berge.

De gauche à droite, du haut vers le bas:
Cheminée, séjour/salle à manger,
salle de bain, intérieur.
À droite: Extérieur avec la vue sur la montagne.

FERME DU BOIS,
CHAMONIX, FRANCE

HIP CHALETS / JAMIE STRACHAN
(INTERIOR DESIGN). PASCAL REVEL
(ARTISAN WORK & RENOVATIONS).
CHALET DE JULES - CHAMONIX
(FURNITURE SUPPLIER).

www.hipchalets.com

Client: Hip Chalets, **Completion:** 2008, **Gross floor area:** 350 m², **Photos:** Jeremy Wilson.

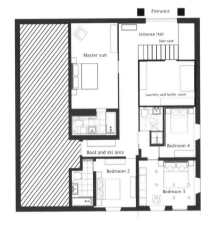

Left: Exterior. Links: Außenansicht. À gauche: Extérieur. | Right: Floor plans. Rechts: Grundrisse. À droite: Plans.

Ferme du Bois was built by Jean Couttet in 1740. It is one of the oldest buildings in the Chamonix valley. Some time before Second World War the house underwent some changes where the hayloft was turned into living quarters and the fireplace was cut to its current position. It was used as a family home for many years and there are stunning authentic antique furniture throughout the house. The rustic structure and history of the chalet have been lovingly maintained, integrating modern features where necessary. Ferme du Bois gives a homely and comfortable atmosphere with an unequalled sense of social space and a perfect location at the foot of Mont Blanc with views of the entire mountain range.

Ferme du Bois wurde 1740 von Jean Couttet errichtet. Das Chalet ist eines der ältesten Bauten im Tal von Chamonix. Bereits vor dem Zweiten Weltkrieg wurde sein Heuboden zu Wohnzwecken umgebaut und der Kamin an seine heutige Stelle gesetzt. In dem viele Jahre als Einfamilienhaus genutzten Gebäude finden sich überall bemerkenswerte antike Möbel. Der rustikale Baukörper und die Geschichte des Chalets wurden liebevoll bewahrt und soweit erforderlich moderne Einbauten integriert. Ferme du Bois verbreitet eine freundliche und behagliche Atmosphäre an einem unvergleichlichen, geselligen Ort am Fuße des Mont Blancs mit Aussichten auf die gesamte Bergkette.

Construit par Jean Couttet en 1740, ce chalet compte parmi les plus anciens de la vallée de Chamonix. Des modifications apportées peu avant la Seconde Guerre mondiale ont consisté en l'aménagement d'un séjour dans l'ancienne grange et la reconstruction de la grande cheminée. Le chalet est resté une maison familiale durant de longues années, comme en témoignent les magnifiques meubles rustiques qu'on y voit encore. Une modernisation a été réalisée récemment avec un profond respect de l'histoire des lieux et de la tradition savoyarde. Aujourd'hui, la Ferme du Bois est une demeure de caractère qui offre un grand confort, des espaces conviviaux d'une qualité remarquable et une vue imprenable sur tout le massif du mont Blanc.

From left to right, from above to below:
Bathroom, bedroom, living room.
Right: Lounge with fireplace.

Von links nach rechts, von oben nach unten:
Badezimmer, Schlafzimmer, Wohnzimmer.
Rechts: Aufenthaltsraum mit Kamin.

De gauche à droite, du haut vers le bas:
Salle de bain, chambre, séjour.
À droite: Séjour avec cheminée.

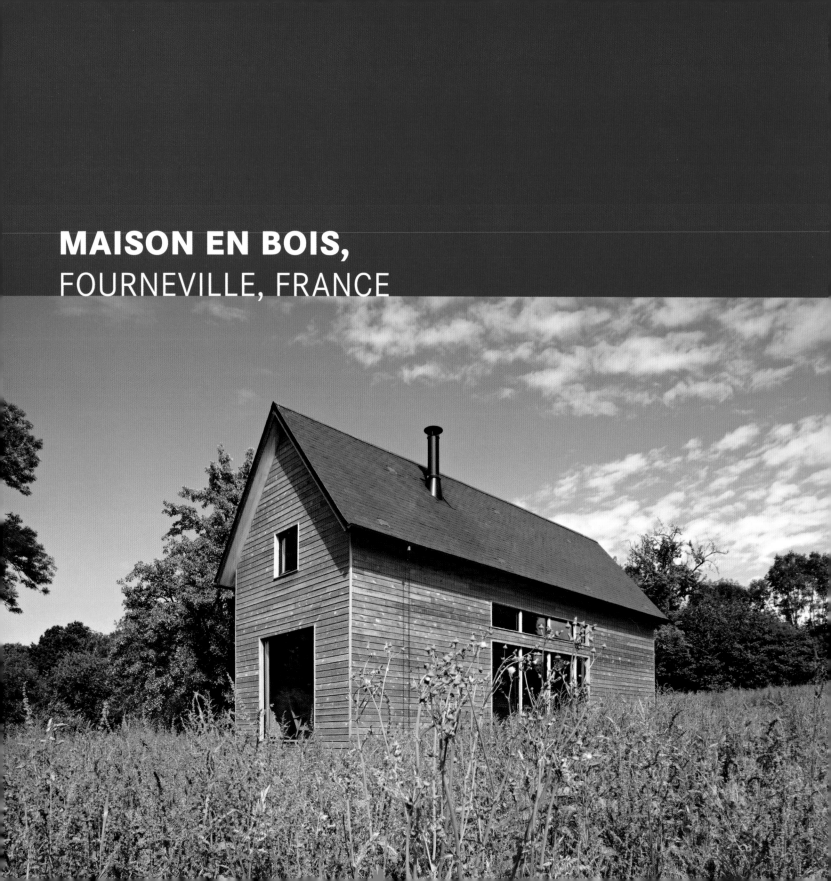

MAISON EN BOIS,
FOURNEVILLE, FRANCE

LODE ARCHITECTURE -
LACOSTE / VINÇON

www.lode-architecture.com
Client: SCI Silent Way, **Completion:** 2007, **Gross floor area:** 90 m², **Photos:** Daniel Moulinet.

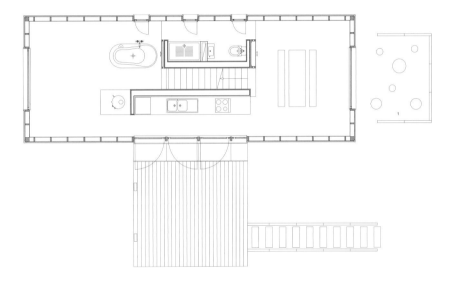

Left: Exterior. Links: Gesamtansicht. À gauche: Vue d'ensemble. | Right: Floor plan. Rechts: Grundriss. À droite: Plan.

This weekend house integrates the latest criteria as regards comfort, cost-saving and environment-friendliness. The users shall come here to appreciate quiet leisure-time together with their friends. The architecture suggests a mountain lodge as well as a ship cabin. The light construction structure offers various community rooms and combines various functions freely: bath tube "with a view" near the oven, elongated kitchen with direct access to the terrace, dormitory with hanging bunks. The monochrome natural materials contrast with the colors of the surrounding meadow. Every room affords selected views on the landscape, thus interconnecting the interior and the exterior.

Bei der Gestaltung dieses modernen Wochenendhauses bestand die Aufgabe der Architekten darin, ein bequemes, kostengünstiges und umweltfreundliches Gebäude zu entwerfen. Das Gebäude aus leichter Bauweise bietet verschiedene Gemeinschaftsräume und eine freie Kombination der Funktionen: Badewanne „mit Aussicht" neben dem Ofen, langgestreckte Küche mit direktem Zugang zur Terrasse, Schlafsaal mit hängenden Liegen. Die einfarbigen, naturbelassenen Materialien bilden einen Gegensatz zur Farbe der umliegenden Wiese. Jeder Raum steht durch gezielte Öffnungen, die eine Wechselwirkung zwischen nah und fern ermöglichen, in Verbindung mit der Landschaft.

Cette maison de week-end est conçue pour un usage intermittent, selon des critères actuels de confort, d'économie et d'impact écologique. L'architecture fait ici référence à des imaginaires multiples : la cabane, le refuge, la cabine de bateau. En résulte une maison de construction légère, qui propose des espaces participatifs et combine librement les programmes : baignoire « avec vue » attenante au poêle, cuisine-façade ouvrant sur la terrasse, dortoir avec couchettes suspendues. Les matériaux bruts forment une palette monochromatique qui s'oppose aux couleurs de la prairie. Chaque espace de la maison invite le paysage par des cadrages choisis, en alternant vues rapprochées et rapports au lointain.

Bathroom. Badezimmer. Salle de bain.

From left to right, from above to below:
Exterior, interior, bathroom.
Right: Second floor.

Von links nach rechts, von oben nach unten:
Außenansicht, Wohnbereich, Badezimmer.
Rechts: Zweites Obergeschoss.

De gauche à droite, du haut vers le bas:
Extérieur, intérieur, salle de bain.
À droite: Vue du niveau supérieur.

NICKY DOBREE INTERIOR DESIGN LIMITED

www.descent.co.uk
Client: Private, **Completion:** 2004, **Gross floor area:** 350 m², **Photos:** John Warburton Lee.

Left: Living room with wooden ceiling. Links: Wohnzimmer mit Holzdecke. À gauche: Séjour avec poutres apparentes. | Right: Floor plans. Rechts: Grundrisse. À droite: Plans.

A chocolate box exterior belies a chic and contemporary interior. "Beyond perfect" is how Victoria Mather summed up La Ferme de Moudon, a 17th century Savoyard farm building transformed into an icon of contemporary design. A minimalist masterpiece, the large open plan living space is instantly calming, blending ancient timbers above with carefully chosen contemporary furnishings below. Light floods in from two vast picture windows, while the uninterrupted views of the national park, pistes and powder fields give the feeling that all you survey is your own.

Hinter einer verspielten Fassade verbirgt sich ein elegantes Inneres. „Mehr als perfekt", so charakterisiert Victoria Mather die Ferme de Moudon. Das savoyardische Wirtschaftsgebäude aus dem 17. Jahrhundert wurde zu einer Ikone zeitgenössischen Designs umgebaut. Als minimalistisches Meisterwerk wirkt der große offene Wohnraum sogleich beruhigend. Altes Holz im oberen Bereich wird mit ausgewählten modernen Mobiliar im unteren Wohnbereich kombiniert. Durch zwei Panoramafenster flutet Licht hinein, während der Blick auf den Nationalpark, die Pisten und die Felder mit Pulverschnee dem Betrachter das Gefühl geben, als schaue er auf sein Eigentum.

« Plus que parfaite » : c'est ainsi que la journaliste Victoria Mather présente la ferme de Moudon, bâtiment savoyard du XVIIe siècle dont l'intérieur a été réaménagé en style contemporain. Le grand séjour est un chef-d'œuvre minimaliste où les poutres d'origine s'allient au mobilier moderne pour créer une atmosphère immédiatement apaisante. Deux grandes fenêtres y ouvrent sur le magnifique paysage du parc naturel, avec les pistes de ski et les champs de poudreuse à portée de la main.

From left to right, from above to below:
Interior view, bedroom, bathroom, hot tub on terrace.
Right: Drawing room with dining area.

Von links nach rechts, von oben nach unten:
Innenansicht, Schlafzimmer, Badezimmer,
Whirlpool auf der Terrasse.
Rechts: Salon mit Essecke.

De gauche à droite, du haut vers le bas:
Intérieur, chambre, salle de bain, baignoire extérieure chauffée.
À droite: Séjour/salle à manger.

CHALET MONTANA,
VAL D'ISÈRE, FRANCE

CLAUDE AMANN

www.descent.co.uk

Client: Private, **Completion:** 2004, **Gross floor area:** 500 m², **Photos:** Dale Shires.

Left: Interior with wooden cladding. Links: Innenbereich mit Holzverkleidung. À gauche: Intérieur avec boiseries. | Right: Floor plans. Rechts: Grundrisse. À droite: Plans.

Arranged over four floors on the side of the slope, every room and terrace shares the same perfect views, including the indoor pool, where one can swim against the jetstream while contemplating the incredible view of snow-capped peaks. The six bedrooms are all ensuite, the sixth of which doubles as a children's bunkroom, a brilliantly conceived wonderland of wood. Upstairs, the split-level main living area is thoughtfully designed to be both spacious and intimate, with soothing muted tones, bespoke furniture, and local stone throughout.

Da alle Zimmer in den vier Geschossen an der Hangseite liegen, verfügen sie über die gleichen Aussichten. Auch aus dem Swimmingpool im Inneren des Gebäudes kann man die fantastische Aussicht auf die schneebedeckten Gipfel genießen. Es beherbergt sechs Schlafzimmer, die jeweils über ein eigenes Bad verfügen. Das Kinderzimmer mit Etagenbetten ist als Zauberland aus Holz konzipiert. Im oberen Geschoss ist der mit versetzten Ebenen ausgeführte Hauptwohnbereich sorgfältig gestaltet, damit er gleichzeitig intim und weitläufig wirkt. Das Interieur bestimmen gedämpfte Töne, maßgefertigte Möbel und lokaler Naturstein.

Ce chalet de quatre étages est construit à flanc de montagne, de sorte que chaque pièce et chaque terrasse bénéficient de vues magnifiques. Il en va de même de la piscine thalasso où l'on peut nager en regardant les sommets enneigés. Les six chambres disposent d'une salle de bain et l'une d'entre elles se double d'une chambre pour les enfants, véritable espace de rêve tout en bois. Le grand séjour sur deux niveaux est très spacieux. Des meubles faits sur mesure s'y associant à des tons apaisants et à un usage intensif de la pierre naturelle pour créer une atmosphère particulièrement intimiste.

From left to right, from above to below:
Detail interior, dining area, bathroom, bedroom.
Right: Bedroom with fireplace.

Von links nach rechts, von oben nach unten:
Innenraumdetail, Essecke, Badezimmer, Schlafzimmer.
Rechts: Schlafzimmer mit offenem Kamin.

De gauche à droite, du haut vers le bas:
Détail de l'intérieur, salle à manger, salle de bain, chambre.
À droite: Chambre avec cheminée.

LE ROCHER,
VAL D'ISÈRE, FRANCE

MICHEL COVAREL

www.descent.co.uk
Client: Private, **Completion:** 2008, **Gross floor area:** 800 m², **Photos:** Jan Baldwin.

Left: Master bedroom. Links: Hauptschlafzimmer. À gauche: Chambre à coucher principale. | Right: Floor plans. Rechts: Grundrisse. À droite: Plans.

The chalet is beautifully finished, mixing a rustic Alpine style with reclaimed wood from Mongolia, intricately carved furnishings and designer pieces, to create the perfect blend of new and old. Le Rocher, which literally translates as "the rock", has been constructed into the mountainside with the natural rock face exposed in the massage room and one of the bathrooms - a spectacular feature! The spacious interior also boasts an indoor swimming pool with jet stream, a Hammam, massage room, a home gym and solarium. A beautiful red cedar hot tub is situated on the balcony.

Das hervorragend ausgeführte Chalet kombiniert einen rustikalen Alpenstil mit Altholz aus der Mongolei, diffizil geschnitztem Mobiliar und Designerstücke, um eine perfekte Mischung aus Alt und Neu zu schaffen. Le Rocher oder „der Felsen" wurde in den Berghang gebaut. Im Massageraum und einem der Badezimmer ist die natürliche Felswand zu sehen – eine spektakuläre Besonderheit. Im großzügigen Innenbereich finden sich außerdem ein Schwimmbecken mit Gegenstrom, ein Hamam, ein Fitnessraum und ein Solarium. Auf dem Balkon steht ein Whirlpool aus Red Cedar.

La décoration intérieure de ce chalet réalise une synthèse exceptionnelle de l'ancien et du moderne, dans la mesure où elle intègre la tradition rustique des Alpes, les boiseries de Mongolie, les meubles sculptés et les éléments design. Comme son nom l'indique, le bâtiment s'adosse directement au rocher, visible de manière spectaculaire dans le salon de massage et l'une des salles de bains. On trouve également à l'intérieur un hammam, un solarium, une salle de fitness et une piscine thalasso, et sur le balcon une baignoire en cèdre chauffée par un poêle à bois.

From left to right, from above to below:
Exterior view, terrace with Jacuzzi, drawing room with fireplace.
Right: Main dining room.

Von links nach rechts, von oben nach unten:
Außenansicht, Terrasse mit Whirlpool, Salon mit Kamin.
Rechts: Esszimmer.

De gauche à droite, du haut vers le bas:
Extérieur, terrasse avec jacuzzi, séjour avec cheminée.
À droite: Salle à manger.

BIG YETI,

VAL D'ISÈRE, FRANCE

www.descent.co.uk
Client: Private, Completion: 2003, Gross floor area: 320 m², Photos: Jeremy Wilson.

Left: Living room with fireplace. Links: Wohnzimmer mit Kamin. À gauche: Séjour avec cheminée. | Right: Floor plans. Rechts: Grundrisse. À droite: Plans.

Located in the highly exclusive Les Carats enclave, the chalet is ski-in/ski-out from the La Face piste. Big Yeti sleeps 10 guests in five beautiful bedrooms, all of which are either ensuite or have private bathrooms. Spanning the entire third floor, the master suite consists of an ensuite bathroom with Jacuzzi bath, dressing room and three private balconies. The spacious drawing room with open fireplace, features soft browns and warm fabrics which blend beautifully with the alpine wood and old stone making it a stylish and authentic mountain retreat.

In der luxuriösen Enklave Les Carats liegt das Chalet unmittelbar an der Piste La Face. Big Yeti bietet Platz für zehn Gäste in fünf wunderschönen Zimmern mit eigenem Bad. Die Master-Suite belegt das gesamte dritte Obergeschoss. Sie enthält ein Badezimmer mit Whirlpool, eine Ankleide und drei private Balkone. Den geräumigen Salon mit offenem Kamin bestimmen sanfte Brauntöne und behagliche Stoffe. Zusammen mit lokalem Holz und altem Naturstein ergeben sie einen eleganten und authentischen Zufluchtsort in den Bergen.

Ce chalet situé dans la copropriété de grand luxe « Les Carats » dispose d'un accès direct aux pistes de ski. Ses cinq chambres pour deux personnes disposent toutes d'une salle de bain. La grande suite qui occupe tout le troisième étage se compose d'une chambre, d'une salle de bain avec jacuzzi, d'un vestiaire et de trois balcons. Dans le vaste séjour avec cheminée, le brun chaleureux des tissus d'ameublement se marie à merveille avec le bois et la pierre des Alpes, créant ainsi une authentique atmosphère de montagne.

From left to right, from above to below:
Bathroom, dining room, lounge, bedroom with open fireplace.
Right: Bedroom with drawing room.

Von links nach rechts, von oben nach unten:
Badezimmer, Esszimmer, Aufenthaltsraum,
Schlafzimmer mit offenem Kamin.
Rechts: Schlafzimmer mit Salon.

De gauche à droite, du haut vers le bas:
Salle de bains, salle à manger, salon,
chambre à coucher avec cheminée.
À droite: Chambre à coucher avec coin salon.

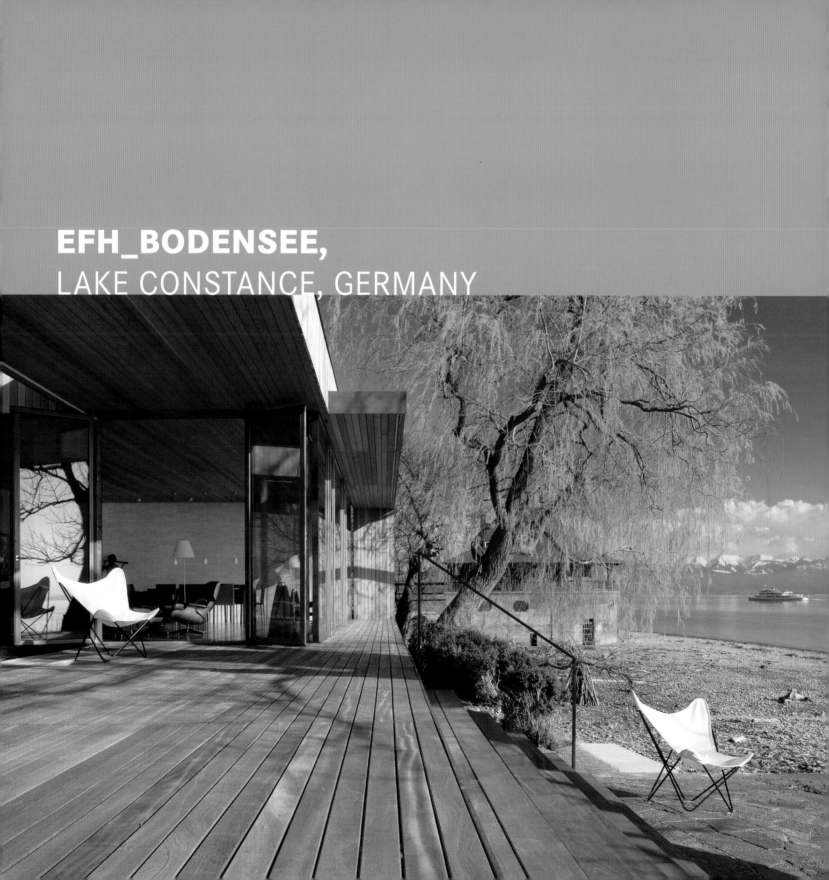

EFH_BODENSEE,
LAKE CONSTANCE, GERMANY

K_M.ARCHITEKTUR DI DANIEL SAUTER

www.k-m-architektur.com

Client: Private, Completion: 2007, Gross floor area: 190 m², Photos: Courtesy of k_m.architektur DI Daniel Sauter.

Left: Beachfront deck. Links: Terrasse mit Strandzugang. À gauche: Façade côté lac. | Right: Ground floor plan. Rechts: Grundriss Erdgeschoss. À droite: Plan du rez-de-chaussée.

The single-floor residential home made of cedar wood was built on a slightly sloping property with direct access to the lake. In the course of time, the patina of the façade is intended to adjust to its natural surroundings. Thus the building discreetly takes a backstage, without disrupting the lake view. The home is divided into two sections. The rear section with a closed façade contains the bedrooms and functional rooms. An open dining and living area with a fireplace faces the lake. The entire length of this side features floor-to-ceiling glazing, offering a fascinating view of the entire Lake Constance.

Das eingeschossige Wohnhaus aus Zedernholz wurde auf einem leicht abfallenden Grundstück mit direktem Seezugang errichtet. Die Fassade soll sich im Laufe der Zeit mit seiner Patina optisch der natürlichen Umgebung anpassen. Das Gebäude tritt somit dezent in den Hintergrund, ohne die Uferansicht zu stören. Das Wohnhaus gliedert sich in zwei Bereiche. Im rückwärtigen Bereich mit einer geschlossen gehaltenen Fassade sind die Schlaf- und Nutzräume untergebracht. Ein offener Wohn- und Essbereich mit Feuerstelle orientiert sich zum See. Diese Seite ist über die gesamte Länge raumhoch verglast und gewährt einen faszinierenden Ausblick über den gesamten Bodensee.

Ce pavillon de plain-pied a été construit juste au bord du lac de Constance. Le revêtement de façade en bardeaux de cèdre est appelé à se patiner avec le temps de sorte que le bâtiment, dont le style se caractérise par une grande retenue, se fondra encore mieux dans l'environnement naturel des rives du lac. L'espace habitable se divise en deux parties : chambres et pièces de service à l'arrière, protégées par une façade hermétique ; séjour/salle à manger avec cheminée du côté de l'eau, un pan de mur entièrement vitré assurant ici un panorama intégral sur le lac de Constance.

From left to right, from above to below:
Glass walls, exterior with path, living room.
Right: Sundeck with glass façade.

Von links nach rechts, von oben nach unten:
Glasfassade, Blick auf die Terrasse, Wohnzimmer.
Rechts: Terrasse mit Glasfassade.

De gauche à droite, du haut vers le bas:
Murs entièrement vitrés, sentier autour de la maison, séjour.
À droite: Terrasse.

SPLIT & ROTATE,
NAOUSSA, EAST VERMION, GREECE

NICOS KALOGIROU

Client: Kostas Lapavitsas, **Completion:** 2008, **Gross floor area:** 143 m², **Photos:** Nicos Kalogirou.

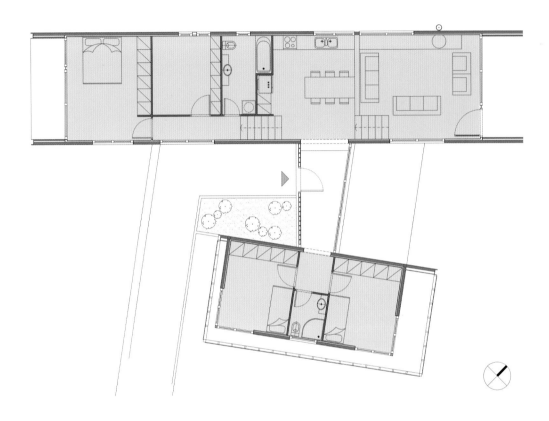

Left: General view. Links: Gesamtansicht. À gauche: Vue d'ensemble. | Right: Floor plan. Rechts: Grundriss. À droite: Plan.

Responding to the spirit of the place, the general layout is austere, with clear geometric elements, industrial aesthetics and dynamic yet controllable tension. The general layout results from the split in two unequal parts: the main residence and the children's pavilion – that are bridged with a transparent, glass passage way. The composition results from the simultaneous rotation of the volumes on two axes according to the topography and the views, thus ensuring, a dialectic composition of the entirety, with clear, relatively independently functioning yet connected parts.

Auf den Stil des Ortes antwortet der Gesamtplan mit einem nüchternen Ausdruck, klaren geometrischen Elementen, Industrieästhetik und einer dynamischen, doch beherrschbaren Spannung. Der Grundriss ist in zwei ungleiche Teile aufgespalten, das Haupthaus und den Kinderpavillon. Beide sind durch einen Glasgang miteinander verbunden. Die ausgeklügelte Komposition resultiert aus der gleichzeitigen Drehung der Baukörper auf zwei Achsen entsprechend der Topografie und den Aussichten. Dadurch ergeben sich eindeutige, relativ unabhängig funktionierende, doch miteinander verknüpfte Teile.

L'architecture est ici en harmonie avec l'esprit des lieux : austère, à base d'éléments géométriques simples, et intégrant un esthétisme industriel et un dynamisme contrôlé. Il s'agit d'un complexe formé de deux unités inégales (le bâtiment principal et l'annexe réservée aux enfants), reliées par un couloir en verre. La composition générale résulte de la rotation des volumes sur deux axes en fonction de la topographie et des vues sur les alentours, avec pour résultat un ensemble clair composé de deux parties relativement indépendantes en dépit de leur interconnexion.

From left to right, from above to below:
Hallway, glazed façade, rear view.
Right: Detail exterior.

Von links nach rechts, von oben nach unten:
Flur, verglaste Fassade, Rückansicht.
Rechts: Außendetail.

De gauche à droite, du haut vers le bas:
Couloir en verre, façade vitrée, face arrière.
À droite: Couloir vu de l'extérieur.

HOUSE RIZZI,
ST. MARTIN IM KOFEL, ITALY

WERNER TSCHOLL ARCHITEKT

www.werner-tscholl.com
Client: Walter Rizzi, **Completion:** 1998, **Gross floor area:** 616 m², **Photos:** Courtesy of Werner Tscholl Architekt.

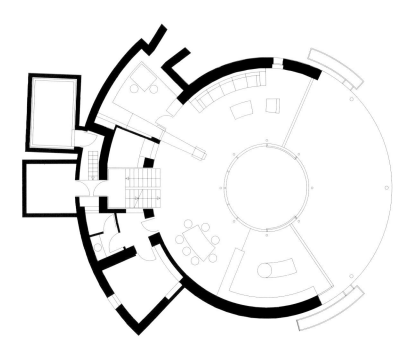

Left: General view with mountain panorama. Links: Gesamtansicht mit Panoramablick. À gauche: La tour dominant la vallée. | **Right:** Ground floor plan. Rechts: Grundriss Erdgeschoss. À droite: Plan du rez-de-chaussée.

The perfectly circular residential home incorporates five floors and is positioned prominently in the vicinity of the mountains. With its old defense tower design, the building resembles a fortress. In addition to its archaic shape, the building is distinguished by its electronically controlled steel drawbridge. The approximately 22-meter high cylinder of the donjon is placed immediately near the precipice with a massive quarry stonewall facing the mountainside, only interrupted by a few narrow windows. The house opens up along its entire height towards the valley. The donjon consists of a double cylinder with a second glass-roof glass barrel at its center, which provides transparent illumination.

Das kreisrunde Wohnhaus beherbergt fünf Stockwerke und steht exponiert am Berg. Mit seiner Konzeption als alter Wehrturm erinnert das Gebäude an eine Burg. Neben der archaischen Form macht die elektronisch gesteuerte Zugbrücke aus Stahl eine Besonderheit dieses Volumens aus. Der etwa 22 Meter hohe Zylinder des Bergfrieds steht hart am Hang und zeigt zur Bergseite eine massive Bruchsteinwand, die nur von einigen schmalen Fenstern durchbrochen ist. Zum Tal hin öffnet sich das Haus in voller Höhe. Der Bergfried besteht aus einem Doppelzylinder in dessen Mitte sich eine zweite Glastonne mit Glasdach befindet, die für Transparenz sorgt.

Ce bâtiment construit à flanc de montagne marie on ne peut mieux archaïsme et modernisme. Il s'agit d'une « tour de guet » de cinq étages pourvue d'un pont-levis en acier à commande électronique. Haut de vingt-deux mètres, cet édifice cylindrique en pierres naturelles présente, face à la montagne, un mur où l'on ne distingue que quelques fenêtres de dimensions réduites. Par contre, le côté qui fait face à la vallée s'ouvre par une large terrasse. Un véritable puits de lumière, aux parois entièrement vitrées et couvert d'une coupole prismatique, assure un bon éclairage naturel de l'intérieur.

Stone façade and sundeck. Steinfassade und Terrasse. La maison en pierres vue d'en bas, du côté de la terrasse.

From left to right, from above to below:
Detail stone wall, pool, fireplace, glazed hallway.
Right: Side view.

Von links nach rechts, von oben nach unten:
Steinfassadendetail, Swimmingpool, Kamin, verglaster Flur.
Rechts: Seitenansicht.

De gauche à droite, du haut vers le bas:
Détail des murs en pierres, piscine, cheminée, couloir vitré.
À droite: Face arrière.

HOUSE TO CATCH THE FOREST,
CHINO-SHI, NAGANO, JAPAN

TEZUKA ARCHITECTS

www.tezuka-arch.com

Client: Private, **Completion:** 2004, **Gross floor area:** 80 m², **Photos:** Katsuhisa Kida / FOTOTECA.

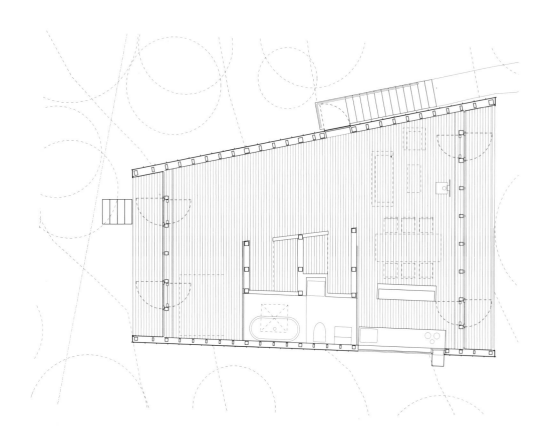

Left: Front view. Links: Vorderansicht. À gauche: Face avant. | Right: Floor plan. Rechts: Grundriss. À droite: Plan.

The House to Catch the Forest is a cottage floating in the middle of red pines that exceed 20 meters in height. To fully appreciate the setting, the house was slightly elevated and designed to offer a view of the treetops. The steep roof was conceived to prevent the accumulation of snow and leaves. The interior is almost totally devoid of partitions, but walls can be pulled on both sides of the bathroom. The center core manages to provide a certain sense of privacy despite the absence of partitions. The House to Catch the Forest merges the concepts of a multifunctional interior and a space that embraces the surrounding landscape.

Dieses kleine Landhaus schwebt zwischen mehr als 20 Meter hohen Rotkiefern. Um die Lage auszunutzen, wurde die Konstruktion angehoben und so entworfen, dass sie Aussichten auf die Baumwipfel gewährt. Ihr steiles Dach soll Ansammlungen von Schnee und Laub verhindern. Innen sind kaum Unterteilungen vorhanden, aber an beiden Seiten des Badezimmers lassen sich Trennwände zuziehen. Trotz der fehlenden Abtrennungen vermittelt die Kernzone eine gewisse Privatsphäre. Bei diesem Haus verschmilzt das Konzept eines multifunktionalen Innerns mit dem eines Raums, der die umgebende Landschaft einbezieht.

House to catch the forest Construite parmi des pins de plus de vingt mètres de haut, cette « maison pour attraper la forêt » repose sur pilotis et dispose de vastes surfaces vitrées permettant aux occupants d'apprécier le site naturel. La forte pente du toit permet d'éviter l'accumulation de neige et d'aiguilles de pin. L'intérieur est décloisonné mais des paravents sont disponibles pour isoler la salle de bain des deux côtés. L'espace central offre une certaine intimité en dépit de son plan ouvert. L'objectif consistait ici à réaliser un habitat multifonctionnel en symbiose avec l'environnement naturel.

From left to right, from above to below:
Bathroom, side view of exterior, interior.
Right: Rear view of exterior.

Von links nach rechts, von oben nach unten:
Badezimmer, Außenansicht, Wohnzimmer mit Kamin.
Rechts: Eingangsansicht.

De gauche à droite, du haut vers le bas:
Salle de bain, maison parmi les arbres, intérieur.
À droite: Face arrière.

HOUSE ON THE MOUNTAINSIDE,
HYOGO, JAPAN

KEIICHI HAYASHI ARCHITECT

www.haya-at.com

Client: Satoshi & Shoko Tanaka, **Completion:** 2005, **Gross floor area:** 96 m², **Photos:** Masao Nishikawa.

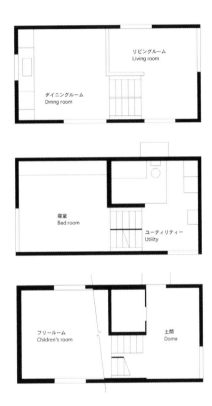

リビングルーム
Living room

ダイニングルーム
Dining room

寝室
Bed room

ユーティリティー
Utility

フリールーム
Children's room

土間
Doma

Left: Exterior surrounded by trees. Links: Gesamtansicht. À gauche: Maison entourée d'arbres. | Right: Floor plans. Rechts: Grundrisse. À droite: Plans.

House on the Mountainside is a mini skyscraper that stacks up the living accommodation. The stacked space allows for spectacular views, framed by large sliding windows that can be drawn across the façade. Six skipping floors are planned alongside the slope. Each floor is designed to be homogenous with the rest of the structure. Only the position of the windows modifies the space. The atmosphere in the house changes as you move from floor to floor, the experience being unique every time — owing to a changing surrounding environment.

Bei dem Haus auf dem Berghang, einem kleinen Wolkenkratzer, sind die Wohnnutzungen übereinandergestapelt. Dadurch bietet es spektakuläre Aussichten, die von großen Schiebefenstern gerahmt werden, welche sich über die Fassade ziehen lassen. Parallel zum Hang entstehen sechs versetzte Geschosse. Da alle Etagen einheitlich gestaltet sind, verändert lediglich die Position der Fenster den Raum. In jedem Geschoss des Hauses herrscht eine andere Atmosphäre. Beim Wechsel der Geschosse erzeugt die sich verändernde Umgebung jedes Mal ein einzigartiges Raumerlebnis.

Construite à flanc de colline, cette maison de six étages toute en hauteur est comme un gratte-ciel résidentiel miniaturisé. De grandes fenêtres coulissantes maximisent l'éclairage naturel et les vues sur le paysage, tout en minimisant l'espace pris à l'intérieur. Chaque étage a été conçu de manière à former un ensemble homogène, la seule différence d'un niveau à l'autre résidant dans la disposition des fenêtres. Chacun dispose néanmoins d'une atmosphère qui lui est propre, précisément du fait de ce rapport toujours renouvelé à l'extérieur.

From left to right, from above to below:
Stairs, interior, exterior.
Right: Bathroom.

Von links nach rechts, von oben nach unten:
Treppe, Interieur, Rückansicht.
Rechts: Badezimmer.

De gauche à droite, du haut vers le bas:
Escalier, intérieur, extérieur.
À droite: Salle de bain.

DRIFT BAY HOUSE,
QUEENSTOWN, NEW ZEALAND

KERR RITCHIE ARCHITECTS

www.kerrritchie.com
Client: Peter Ritchie & Bronwen Kerr, **Completion:** 2007, **Gross floor area:** 270 m², **Photos:** Paul McCredie.

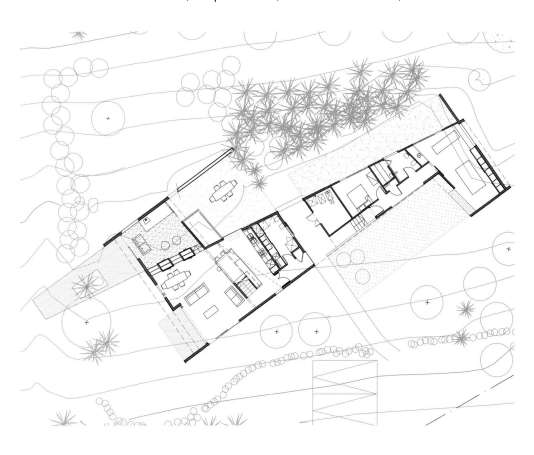

Left: Rear view. Links: Rückansicht. À gauche: Face arrière. | Right: Site plan. Rechts: Lageplan. À droite: Plan de situation.

This family home was designed as a single fluid form that reclines into the sloping landscape on the edge of Lake Wakatipu. The long black form shifts and expands to suit the sun, the occupants' needs and the site. The roof and walls of the house are clad in black steel and timber weatherboards. The entry is through a hole punched in the middle creating a courtyard. This allows visitors to enter either the family home to the north or the studio/guest wing to the south. The interior is intended to have the resilience of an institutional building. Space shifts, as well as form, up and down to create spaces that move from snug to lofty and back again.

Dieses Einfamilienhaus lehnt sich als eine einzige flie-ßende Form an die abschüssige Landschaft am Ufer des Sees Wakatipu. Die lange Gebäudegestalt verschiebt sich und dehnt sich aus, um der Sonne, den Bedürfnissen der Bewohner und dem Grundstück zu folgen. Dach und Wände des Baus sind mit schwarzem Stahl und Stulpschalungsbrettern verkleidet. Erschlossen wird das Gebäude durch einen Hohlraum in der Mitte des Hauses, der einen Hof schafft. Dadurch können Besucher entweder die Wohnunterkunft im Norden oder den Studio-/Gästeflügel im Süden betreten. Innen soll das Haus ebenso haltbar sein wie ein Institutsgebäude. Das Auf und Ab des Baus führt zu unterschiedlichen Räumen und Formen.

Les formes fluides de cette maison ont été conçues de manière à s'adapter à la pente qui descend jusqu'au bord du lac de Wakatipu, ainsi qu'à l'ensoleillement et aux besoins des occupants. Le toit et les murs sont recouverts de plaques d'acier et de bardeaux en bois brut résistant aux intempéries. Deux volumes en L sont disposés de part et d'autre d'une entrée centrale qui donne accès à l'aile nord réservée à la famille, ainsi qu'à l'aile sud qui abrite un atelier et des chambres d'amis. L'intérieur se caractérise par son élasticité exceptionnelle, puisque des décalages, associés à des différences de niveaux, y créent divers espaces flexibles.

Exterior with patio and entry. Außenansicht mit Hof und Eingang. Vue panoramique figurant la terrasse et l'escalier menant à l'entrée principale.

From left to right, from above to below:
View of surrounding landscape, bay view, bathroom, kitchen.
Right: Interior with fireplace.

Von links nach rechts, von oben nach unten:
Gesamtansicht, Panoramablick, Badezimmer, Küche.
Rechts: Wohnzimmer mit Kamin.

De gauche à droite, du haut vers le bas:
La maison dans son environnement naturel, vue de la maison et
de la baie, salle de bain, cuisine.
À droite: Séjour avec poêle.

ATRIUM CABIN ON VARDEHAUGEN,
ÅFJORD KOMMUNE, NORWAY

SIVILARKITEKT MNAL HÅKON MATRE AASARØD / FANTASTIC NORWAY AS

www.fantasticnorway.no

Client: Knut Aasarød / Synnøve Matre, **Completion:** 2008, **Gross floor area:** 77 m², **Photos:** Arne Michal Paulsen.

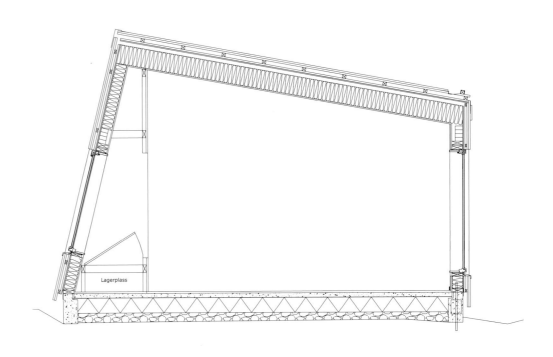

Lagerplass

Left: General view. Links: Gesamtansicht. À gauche: Vue d'ensemble. | Right: Section. Rechts: Schnitt. À droite: Vue en coupe.

The project is a coastal cabin 35 meters above sea level with a panoramic view in virtually all directions. The building is inspired by the traditional Norwegian farmyard, in which flexible half-climatic outside spaces and a clear social organization are the leading principles. The planning of the cabin was executed during a year of regular trips to Vardehaugen to get the most complete impression of the varying climatic conditions affecting the property. To provide maximum protection for the cabin, the black roof folds in and becomes wall surfaces towards the most exposed directions.

Das Küstenhäuschen steht 35 Meter über dem Meeresspiegel und bietet Panoramaaussichten in praktisch alle Richtungen. Der Bau ist von einem traditionellen norwegischen Wirtschaftshof inspiriert, bei dem flexible, halb offene Außenräume und eine klare soziale Organisation die Hauptprinzipien sind. Geplant wurde das Häuschen während der einjährigen regelmäßigen Fahrten nach Vardehaugen, um sich von den variierenden Klimaverhältnissen am Standort ein genaues Bild zu machen. Für einen maximalen Schutz des Häuschens ist das schwarze Dach nach innen gefaltet und wird an den Wetterseiten zur Wandoberfläche.

Cette maison construite sur une falaise haute de trente-cinq mètres offre une vue panoramique sur la montagne et la mer toute proche. Des zones extérieures semi-climatiques et une organisation claire de l'espace l'inscrivent dans la tradition des fermes norvégiennes. Les architectes ont conçu le bâtiment après avoir séjourné sur place à plusieurs reprises durant toute une année afin d'avoir une impression d'ensemble des conditions climatiques qui règnent sur cette île située par-delà le cercle polaire. C'est ainsi qu'afin d'offrir une protection maximale face à la rigueur du climat, ils ont opté pour un toit se transformant progressivement en mur sur la face la plus exposée aux intempéries.

Front entrance. Vordereingang. Façade du côté de l'entrée.

From left to right, from above to below:
Exterior through grass, deck, living area, exterior.
Right: Interior.

Von links nach rechts, von oben nach unten:
Außenansicht, Terrasse, Wohnzimmer, Fassade.
Rechts: Wohnbereich mit Kamin.

De gauche à droite, du haut vers le bas:
La maison dans son environnement de roche et d'herbe,
terrasse, séjour, vue de l'extérieur.
À droite: Séjour avec cheminée.

PREIKESTOLEN FJELLSTUE,
JØRPERLAND, NORWAY

HELEN & HARD AS

www.hha.no
Client: Stavanger Turistforening (Stavanger Trekking Association), **Completion:** 2008, **Gross floor area:** 1,286 m², **Photos:** Jiri Havran, Sune Eriksen (160 r. b.).

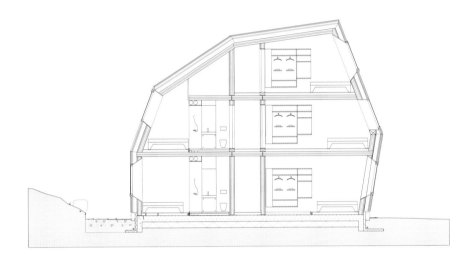

Left: Side view of exterior. Links: Seitenansicht. À gauche: Chalet dominant le lac. | Right: Section. Rechts: Schnitt. À droite: Vue en coupe.

The client is Stavanger Turistforening, an association that facilitates hiking in the mountains through small cabins open to all. They needed a new building to serve the rapidly increasing amount of tourists hiking to Pulpit Rock. It was clear that the old cabin, built 1947, with bunk beds and a shared shower in the hallway did not meet modern standards. The client's wish was to create an accommodation building with upgraded bathroom facilities but still modest. The building features a restaurant with capacity of 100 guests, a small conference room, universal access and is built with environmentally friendly materials.

Stavanger Turistforening ist eine Vereinigung, die das Wandern in den Bergen durch kleine, allgemein zugängliche Hütten unterstützt. Um der schnell wachsenden Anzahl der Wanderer zum Preikestolen-Felsen gerecht zu werden, sollte ein neues Gebäude gebaut werden. Das alte, 1947 erbaute Holzhaus entsprach mit Etagenbetten und einer gemeinsamen Dusche im Gang nicht mehr dem modernen Standard. Der Neubau sollte bessere, doch weiterhin bescheidene Sanitäreinrichtungen aufweisen. Zum Gebäude gehören ein Restaurant für 100 Gäste, ein kleiner Konferenzraum und ein Café. Es ist außerdem mit umweltfreundlichen Materialien gebaut.

Le commanditaire de ce chalet est une association qui cherche à promouvoir la randonnée en montagne. Le bâtiment a été construit en remplacement d'un refuge datant de 1947 dont les lits gigognes et la douche commune dans le couloir ne correspondaient plus aux attentes des touristes d'aujourd'hui. Le client souhaitait un édifice plus moderne mais qui restât simple, tout en étant doté d'une petite salle de conférence et d'un restaurant pour une centaine de personnes. Le cahier des charges prévoyait par ailleurs la réalisation d'une route pour tous véhicules et imposait l'utilisation de matériaux écologiques.

Exterior with façade detail. Eingangsbereich. Façade en bois.

From left to right, from above to below:
Bedroom, dining area, living area, exterior.
Right: Bedroom and bathroom.

Von links nach rechts, von oben nach unten:
Schlafzimmer, Esszimmer, Aufenthaltsraum, Gesamtansicht.
Rechts: Schlaf- und Badezimmer.

De gauche à droite, du haut vers le bas:
Chambre, salle à manger, séjour, vue d'ensemble.
À droite: Les chambres et la salle de bain.

SUMMERHOUSE INSIDE OUT
PAPPER, HVALER ISLANDS, NORWAY

REIULF RAMSTAD ARCHITECTS OSLO

www.reiulframstadarkitekter.no

Client: Architect MNAL Reiulf D. Ramstad, **Completion:** 2006, **Gross floor area:** 80 m², **Photos:** Roberto di Tirani.

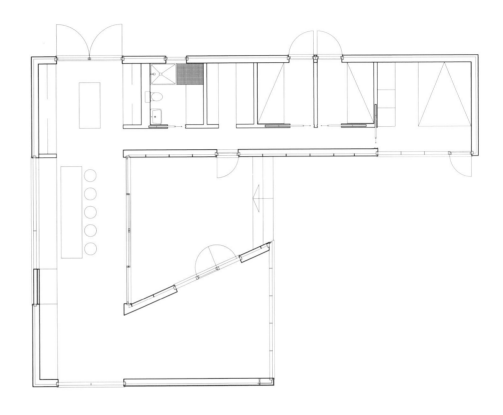

Left: Exterior from below. Links: Talansicht. À gauche: La maison vue d'en bas. | Right: Floor plan. Rechts: Grundriss. À droite: Plan.

The house is beautifully situated on the top of a hill overlooking the ocean and the horizon, placed in the midst of an uncultivated landscape on a small peninsula. The design of the house allows a close interaction with the surrounding nature and the beautiful scenery. It provides a feeling of being outdoors when inside. The small scale of the house together with the use of wooden materials that will gradually develop a grey patina allows the project to interact and fit in with the existing shape and natural colors of the surrounding landscape. At the same time the design contrast with the traditional building practice of the area.

Das schön gelegene Haus auf einem Hügel überblickt den Ozean und den Horizont. Es steht auf einer kleinen Halbinsel inmitten einer landwirtschaftlich ungenutzten Fläche. Der Entwurf des Hauses ermöglicht einen engen Kontakt zur umgebenden Natur und zur prächtigen Landschaft. Innen stellt sich das Gefühl ein, draußen zu sein. Aufgrund seiner kleinen Größe und der Holzmaterialien, die im Laufe der Zeit eine graue Patina annehmen, passt sich das Haus der Form und den natürlichen Farben der umliegenden Landschaft an und fügt sich ihr ein. Gleichzeitig kontrastiert der Entwurf mit der regionalen traditionellen Bauweise.

Cette petite maison est située sur une presqu'île inculte, au sommet d'une colline avec vue sur l'océan. Elle a été conçue de manière à mettre l'architecture en interaction avec la beauté du site naturel, et à créer d'étroits rapports entre l'intérieur et l'extérieur. Cela d'autant plus que l'enveloppe en bois est appelée à se patiner avec le temps et à prendre une teinte grise en harmonie avec la nature environnante. Le bâtiment se distingue néanmoins par rapport aux constructions traditionnelles de la région.

From left to right, from above to below:
Bedroom, deck.
Right: Exterior.

Von links nach rechts, von oben nach unten:
Schlafzimmer, Außenbereich.
Rechts: Gesamtansicht.

De gauche à droite, du haut vers le bas:
Chambre, terrasse.
À droite: Vue d'ensemble.

FARM HOUSE,
TOTEN, NORWAY

JARMUND/VIGSNÆS AS
ARCHITECTS MNAL

www.jva.no
Client: Ane Kristin Rogstad and Trond Nygård, **Completion:** 2008, **Gross floor area:** 165 m², **Photos:** Nils Petter Dale.

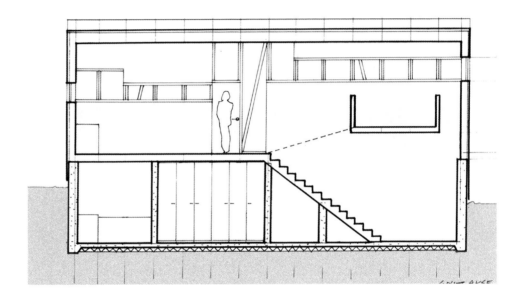

Left: Rear entry. Links: Eingangsbereich. À gauche: Entrée sur la face arrière. | Right: Section. Rechts: Schnitt. À droite: Vue en coupe.

This is a small house for two historians and their children, overlooking lake Mjøsa at an abandoned farm which they have inherited. The 100 years old cladding of the old barn was recycled for both the exterior cladding and terraces of the new house. Some of the old planks are cut with a varied with at the root of the tree compared to the top. These diagonals are used to adjust the horizontality of the cladding towards the sloping lines of the ground and the angle of the roof. The spatial complexity, exposed construction, and material simplicity of the barn has also inspired and informed the new architecture in a wider sense.

Dieses kleine Haus für eine vierköpfige Familie überblickt den See Mjøsa auf einer von ihnen geerbten, ehemaligen Farm. Die 100 Jahre alte Verkleidung der Scheune wurde für die Außenbeplankung und die Terrassen des Neubaus wiederverwendet. Einige der alten Planken sind an der Wurzel des Baumes im Vergleich zu seiner Krone unterschiedlich breit geschnitten. Mit ihnen wird die horizontale Verkleidung zum Geländegefälle und zum Dachwinkel hin ausgeglichen. Die räumliche Komplexität, die exponierte Konstruktion und die einfachen Materialien der Scheune haben die neue Architektur auch im weiteren Sinne inspiriert und geprägt.

Deux historiens qui avaient hérité d'une ferme abandonnée dominant un lac ont chargé les architectes de construire une annexe pour eux et leurs enfants. Le bois de l'ancienne grange, plus que centenaire, a été réutilisé pour le bardage du nouveau bâtiment. Certains bardeaux, dont la forme triangulaire reflète encore le profil de l'arbre duquel ils proviennent, ont été utilisés pour les côtés du bâtiment au niveau du toit. Le résultat est une annexe d'un style architectural novateur, qui associe la complexité spatiale à la simplicité des matériaux, tout en révélant certains détails de la structure porteuse.

Exterior. Gesamtansicht. Vue du bâtiment ancien et de l'annexe.

From left to right, from above to below:
Side view of exterior, looking down into first floor,
hallway, kitchen.
Right: Stairs to upper floor.

Von links nach rechts, von oben nach unten:
Seitenansicht, Blick ins Wohnzimmer, Flur, Küche.
Rechts. Treppe.

De gauche à droite, du haut vers le bas:
L'annexe vue d'en bas, vue plongeante sur le
rez-de-chaussée, vestibule avec poêle, cuisine.
À droite: Rampe et poêle.

HOUSE IN THE ANDES,
SIERRA MORENA, ANTIOQUIA, HUAROCHIRÍ, PERU

JUAN CARLOS DOBLADO

Client: Private, **Completion:** 2008, **Gross floor area:** 438 m², **Photos:** Courtesy of Juan Carlos Doblado.

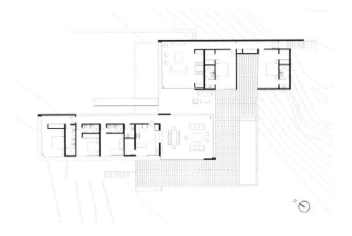

Left: Exterior view with mountains. Links: Gesamtansicht mit Bergpanorama. À gauche: Villa avec les Andes en toile de fond. | Right: Plan. Rechts: Grundriss. À droite: Plan.

Two concrete volumes with great views to the Andes. The house is set on the top of a sloping field. The program is organized in two parallel and horizontal outdated volumes, based on a simple geometry, where the interior is as important as the exterior. The courtyard entry articulates both volumes under one cover and provides a visual opening of the mountains surrounding the valley. In both volumes transparency is what dominates it. Each room has one side covered entirely in glass, so the landscape forms part of the interior space and expands it.

Zwei Betonvolumen gewähren grandiose Aussichten auf die Anden. Das Haus steht auf einem abfallenden Gelände. Sein Programm ist in zwei parallele und horizontale Baukörper organisiert, deren einfache Geometrie Innen- und Außenbereichen die gleiche Bedeutung beimisst. Der Hofeingang verbindet beide Volumen gliedartig unter einem Schutzdach und sorgt für eine optische Öffnung der Berge um das Tal. Beide Baukörper zeichnen sich durch Transparenz aus. Da jedes Zimmer eine vollständig verglaste Seite aufweist, bildet die Landschaft einen Teil des Innenraums und dehnt ihn aus.

Deux volumes en béton sont disposés à angle droit sur un terrain en légère pente, avec les Andes en toile de fond. Toutes les pièces sont au même niveau et s'ouvrent largement sur l'extérieur grâce à de vastes surfaces vitrées qui assurent un bon éclairage de l'intérieur. Du fait de la pente du terrain, le bâtiment qui repose sur des pilotis se trouve en porte-à-faux partiel.

Night view with view to swimming pool. Glasfassade mit Blick auf den Swimmingpool. Surfaces vitrées donnant sur la terrasse et la piscine.

From left to right, from above to below:
Entrance, interior, exterior.
Right: Living room with free-standing fireplace.

Von links nach rechts, von oben nach unten:
Eingang, Wohnzimmer, Gesamtansicht.
Rechts: Wohnzimmer mit freistehendem Kamin.

De gauche à droite, du haut vers le bas:
Villa avec rampe d'accès, vue de l'intérieur, vue d'ensemble.
À droite: Séjour/salle à manger avec poêle.

HOUSE R,
RIBČEV LAZ, BOHINJ, SLOVENIA

BEVK PEROVIĆ ARHITEKTI

www.bevkperovic.com

Client: Private, **Completion:** 2008, **Gross floor area:** 236 m², **Photos:** Miran Kambic.

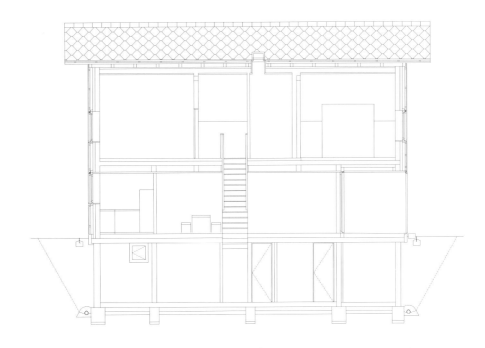

Left: Exterior. Links: Vorderansicht. À gauche: Face avant. | Right: Section. Rechts: Schnitt. À droite: Vue en coupe.

This typical Alpine, yet contemporary vacation home boasts a steep-sloping roofline atop a simple cube base. The entire house was wrapped in wood planks which, when shut, cover the entire structure, as well as windows and doors. This modern minimal exterior is complemented by an equally simple interior with large windows, a bright and spacious layout, and a white palette accented by naturally finished woods. A main staircase divides both, the individual living areas in this open-concept layout, but also connects one floor to the next.

Diese typische, jedoch zeitgenössische Berghütte wartet mit einer steilen Dachsilhouette über einem einfachen Kubus auf. Das rundum mit Holz beplankte Haus ist bei geschlossenen Türen und Fenstern gänzlich mit Holz bedeckt. Das moderne, zurückhaltende Äußere wird durch ein schlichtes Inneres mit großen Fenstern, einem klaren, großzügigen Grundriss und einer weißen Farbpalette, akzentuiert von natürlich bearbeiteten Hölzern, ergänzt. Eine Haupttreppe unterteilt nicht nur die einzelnen Wohnbereiche dieses offenen Grundrisskonzepts, sondern verbindet auch die Geschosse miteinander.

À la fois fidèle à la tradition des chalets alpins et résolument contemporaine, cette maison de vacances se présente sous la forme d'un simple cube couvert d'un toit à deux pentes assez pointu. Elle est entièrement réalisée en bois, y compris les volets, de sorte qu'elle prend un aspect parfaitement hermétique lorsque ceux-ci sont fermés. L'intérieur s'harmonise parfaitement à cette façade minimaliste et moderne par ses pièces vastes et bien éclairées, où le blanc domine et s'allie à des tons de bois brut. Un escalier rythme ce concept d'intérieur ouvert en interconnectant les différents étages.

From left to right, from above to below:
Exterior, interior with stairs, dining room,
alternative view of exterior.
Right: Side view of exterior.

Von links nach rechts, von oben nach unten:
Gesamtansicht; Wohnzimmer mit Treppe in das zweite
Obergeschoss, Essecke, Ansicht mit geschlossenen Fensterläden
Rechts: Seitenansicht.

De gauche à droite, du haut vers le bas:
Face arrière, deux vues du séjour avec escalier, face avant avec
toutes les ouvertures fermées.
À droite: Vue latérale.

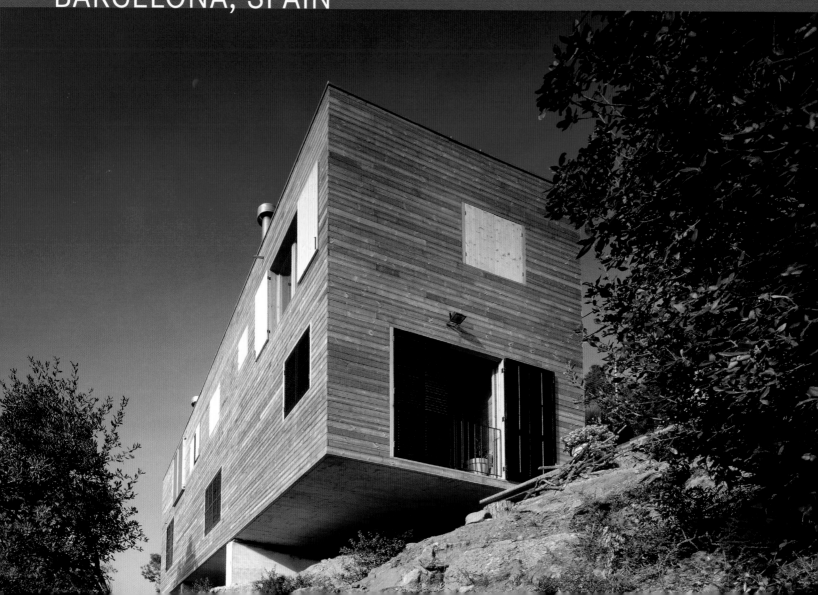

HOUSE 205,
BARCELONA, SPAIN

H ARQUITECTES (DAVID LORENTE, JOSEP RICART, XAVIER ROS, ROGER TUDÓ)

www.harquitectes.com

Client: Fransesc Ortega & Maria Farriol, **Completion:** 2008, **Gross floor area:** 132 m², **Photos:** Starp Estudi.

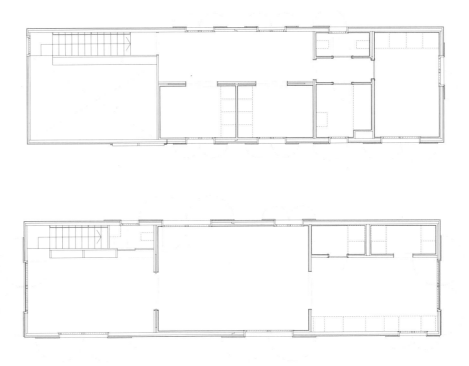

Left: Exterior view from below. Links: Talansicht. À gauche: La maison vue d'en bas. | Right: Floor plans. Rechts: Grundrisse. À droite: Plans.

The setting of the project is a plot with steep slopes and a great amount of trees and bushes. The aim is building a house without causing any serious impacts on the land. The house is built on a natural rocky platform, which is used as either the exit or the garden of the house. The only uneven area is the path ramp, which crosses the piece of land diagonally. The inner layout of the house is based on a lineal sequence of rooms of different proportions linked to the structure. There are great sliding opened areas, which provide both harmony and versatility.

Das Haus steht auf einem Grundstück mit steilen Hängen und zahlreichen Bäumen und Büschen. Es sollte sich nicht nachteilig auf seine Umgebung auswirken. Die natürliche Felsplattform, auf der das Haus errichtet ist, wird entweder als Ausgang oder als Garten genutzt. Der einzig unebene Bereich ist eine Rampe, die das Areal diagonal durchquert. Im Haus reihen sich unterschiedlich proportionierte Räume aneinander und sind mit dem Tragwerk verbunden. Große offene Bereiche mit Schiebeelementen sorgen für Harmonie und Flexibilität.

Cette maison a été construite sur un terrain en pente fortement boisé en veillant à minimiser l'impact sur l'environnement. Elle repose sur un socle rocheux qui constitue une terrasse naturelle à laquelle on accède par un sentier qui part de la route située plus haut. Le plan intérieur correspond à une succession linéaire de pièces de tailles différentes en rapport avec la structure générale. De grandes portes-fenêtres coulissantes assurent un éclairage harmonieux de l'intérieur et permettent un usage polyvalent de l'espace.

Left: Living area. Links: Wohnzimmer. Gauche: Séjour. Right: Study. Rechts: Arbeitszimmer. À droite: Bureau.

From left to right, from above to below:
Exterior from above, living area, deck.
Right: Rear view of exterior.

Von links nach rechts, von oben nach unten:
Gesamtansicht, Kinderzimmer, Terrasse.
Rechts: Rückansicht.

De gauche à droite, du haut vers le bas:
La maison vue d'en haut, séjour, terrasse.
À droite: Face arrière.

GURINER STÜBLI,
BOSCO GURIN, TICINO, SWITZERLAND

EOB.CH - ARTDESIGNARCHITEKTUR - EDUARD OTTO BAUMANN

www.artdesignarchitektur.ch
Client: Raffaele & Claudia Sartori-Feuz, **Completion:** 2007, **Gross floor area:** 72 m², **Photos:** Eduard Otto Baumann.

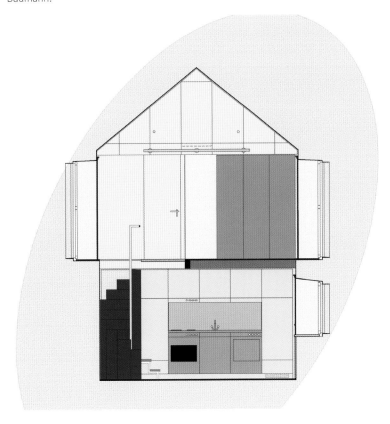

Left: General view. Links: Gesamtansicht. À gauche: Vue d'ensemble. | Right: Section. Rechts: Schnitt. À droite: Vue en coupe.

The Guriner Stübli is located in Bosco Gurin the highest village of the Canton, at 1,506 meters above sea level. The architecture of the house features typical characteristics of the alpine region wood and rock, integrated in the façades. The basic design idea was the innovative use of "boxes" as elements injected into the old space, using minimal interventions. On the ground floor is located the kitchen with the living room. Bedrooms, bathrooms and storage are on the upper floor, with a multipurpose space under the roof.

Das Guriner Stübli liegt in Bosco-Gurin, dem höchsten Dorf des Kantons auf einer Höhe von 1.506 Meter über dem Meeresspiegel. Die Architektur des Hauses zeigt die für die Alpenregion typischen Holz- und Felselemente an der Fassade. Wesentlicher Entwurfsgedanke waren innovativ genutzte, im alten Raum eingefügte „Boxen" und minimale Eingriffe. Das Erdgeschoss beherbergt die Küche mit dem Wohnzimmer. Schlafräume, Bäder und Abstellflächen befinden sich im Obergeschoss und unter dem Dach ist ein Mehrzweckraum untergebracht.

Ce chalet est situé à Bosco Gurin, village du canton du Tessin le plus haut perché (1506 mètres d'altitude). Les façades, typiques de la région alpine, associent le bois et la pierre. Des travaux de rénovation ont été réalisés récemment en intégrant des « boîtes » aux aménagements intérieurs d'origine de manière à minimiser les interventions. La cuisine et le séjour occupent le rez-de-chaussée, tandis que les chambres, les salles de bain et un débarras sont au premier étage et qu'un nouvel espace multifonctionnel se trouve sous les combles.

Amåål, ech ha düä no wå ts Müami in Wertschåft ggwaarchut, sen tü'ssna frèmm Ggèscht ggsutzti ggsin. A Familja met zwej Chenn, eis gånz as chlijs, im Waagali, un ts åndra appu drijjaarigs. Un tè escht isch Eechi varbijggånga un hèt met dèm Büartschi zèllt. As escht as frintlich's ggsin un hèt-mu öw Fåcht gga. Un tè hèt's ufum Waagal'zeichud un hèt-mu ggseit: Mir hänn au no-n-el Buschi! Dar Eechi escht pleba un hèt-mu ggseit: Dås escht doch ggheis Buschi, dås escht doch as Chenn!

Buschu
Buscha /
Buschana
*Kosewort
für die Kuh,
Kinderwort*
Buschi /

Buschalu (f)
Buschala /
Buschali -
Chüa

ts Buschi
måchu
*auf allen
en
echen*

From left to right, from above to below:
Front façade, storage wall, kitchen, interior.
Right: Multipurpose area.

Von links nach rechts, von oben nach unten:
Vorderfassade, Abstellraum, Küche, Treppe.
Rechts: Mehrzweckbereich.

De gauche à droite, du haut vers le bas:
Face avant, débarras, cuisine, escalier.
À droite: Espace multifonctionnel.

NEW BUILDING IN BRIONE S.M.,
BRIONE, SWITZERLAND

MARKUS WESPI JÉRÔME DE MEURON ARCHITEKTEN BSA

www.wespidemeuron.ch
Client: Private, **Completion:** 2005, **Gross floor area:** 155 m², **Photos:** Hannes Henz, Architekturfotograf.

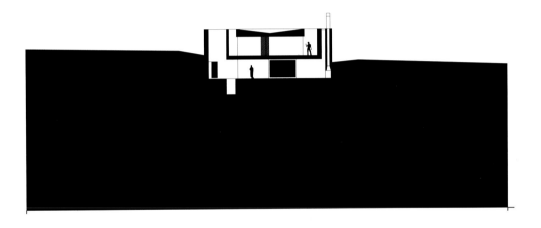

Left: Exterior with stone façade. Links: Steinfassade. À gauche: Façade en pierres. | Right: Section. Rechts: Schnitt. À droite: Vue en coupe.

With a view of the town, lake and mountains the new building is located in a densely populated villa district above Locarno. The design practices constraint for the issue of building in the chaos of urban development. For this reason, the classical attributes of a house were not applied. Only two simply shaped, offset stone cubes constitute the structure that emerges in fractions from the mountain. They are more part of the landscape than the district. The living spaces are created by hollowing out the structure, which permits light to enter from the interior courtyards.

Der Neubau befindet sich mit Sicht auf Stadt, See und Berge in einem dicht bebauten Villenquartier über Locarno. Der Entwurf reagiert mit Zurückhaltung auf das Thema Bauen im städtebaulichen Chaos. Aus diesem Grund wurde auf die Verwendung von Attributen eines klassischen Hauses verzichtet. Lediglich zwei einfach geschnittene, gegenseitig versetzte steinerne Kuben bilden den Baukörper und arbeiten sich bruchstückartig aus dem Berg heraus. Dabei sind sie eher der Landschaft als dem Quartier zugehörig. Die Wohnräume entstehen durch das Prinzip der Aushöhlung, das Licht über die Innenhöfe eindringen lässt.

Cette maison avec vue sur la ville, le lac et les montagnes a été récemment construite dans un quartier résidentiel périphérique de Locarno. Les architectes ont apporté ici une solution empreinte de retenue au problème de la construction dans le chaos urbain. Renonçant aux attributs classiques des maisons d'habitation, ils ont positionné à flanc de montagne deux cubes en pierres dépourvus d'ornements qui semblent plus tournés vers la nature que vers la ville. Les espaces habitables, gagnés en décaissant la montagne, bénéficient d'un bon éclairage naturel grâce à des cours intérieures.

Left: Interior view. Links: Innenansicht. À gauche: Intérieur. Right: Living area with fireplace. Rechts: Sitzgruppe mit Kamin. À droite: Séjour avec cheminée.

From left to right, from above to below:
Interior detail, path with exterior, rooftop view,
view to swimming pool,
Right: Kitchen and dining area.

Von links nach rechts, von oben nach unten:
Innendetail, Zufahrt, Aussicht,
Blick auf den Swimmingpool.
Rechts: Küche mit Panoramablick.

De gauche à droite, du haut vers le bas:
Détail de l'intérieur, chemin d'accès, vue du toit,
vue sur la piscine.
À droite: Cuisine/salle à manger avec vue panoramique.

TIVOLI LODGE,
DAVOS, SWITZERLAND

TARCISI MAISSEN

www.descent.co.uk
Client: Private, **Completion:** 2007, **Gross floor area:** 700 m², **Photos:** Dan Duchars.

Left: Entrance view. Links: Eingangsansicht. À gauche: Façade d'entrée. | Right: Floor plans. Rechts: Grundrisse. À droite: Plans.

The traditional exterior belies a chic and contemporary interior with more than 700 square meters of living space and sensational views from the south-facing windows towards the highest peaks of the Engadine. Tivoli sleeps up to 16 guests in superlative style, with two master bedroom suites, four further bedrooms, plus four more single beds in a delightful children's bunk room, if required. It is perfect for relaxing too, the spa complex houses a relaxation area and hot tub, not to mention a sensational indoor pool, complete with jet stream and a waterfall tumbling into the shallows.

Das traditionelle Äußere verbirgt ein elegantes und modernes Inneres mit mehr als 700 Quadratmetern Wohnraum und sensationellen Aussichten aus den Südfenstern zu den höchsten Gipfeln des Engadins. Tivoli kann bis zu 16 Gäste beherbergen. Vorhanden sind zwei Hauptschlafzimmer, vier weitere Schlafräume sowie vier Etagenbetten in einem Zimmer für Kinder. Zum Entspannen ist das Chalet ausgestattet mit einem Spa-Bereich, in dem sich eine Ruhezone mit Whirlpool, ein aufsehenerregendes Schwimmbecken mit Gegenstrom und ein Wasserfall befinden.

Le chic contemporain se cache derrière une apparence traditionnelle dans ce chalet qui dispose d'une surface habitable de plus de sept cents mètres carrés et offre des vues magnifiques sur les plus hauts sommets de l'Engadine. Conçu pour recevoir jusqu'à seize personnes, le bâtiment abrite deux chambres de maître, quatre chambres de deux personnes et une chambre d'enfants avec quatre couchettes. Les équipements de confort incluent un espace de relaxation, une baignoire extérieure chauffée et une magnifique piscine thalasso avec cascade intégrée.

Front view. Vorderansicht. Façade principale.

From left to right, from above to below:
Entrance hall, drawing room, children's bunk room.
Right: Swimming pool.

Von links nach rechts, von oben nach unten:
Eingangshalle, Empfangsraum, Kinderzimmer.
Rechts: Swimmingpool.

De gauche à droite, du haut vers le bas:
Vestibule, séjour, chambre des enfants.
À droite: Piscine intérieure.

SCHUDEL HOUSE,
FELDIS/VEULDEN, SWITZERLAND

www.oos.com

Client: Private, Completion: 2002, Gross floor area: 222 m², Photos: Dominique Marc Wehrli.

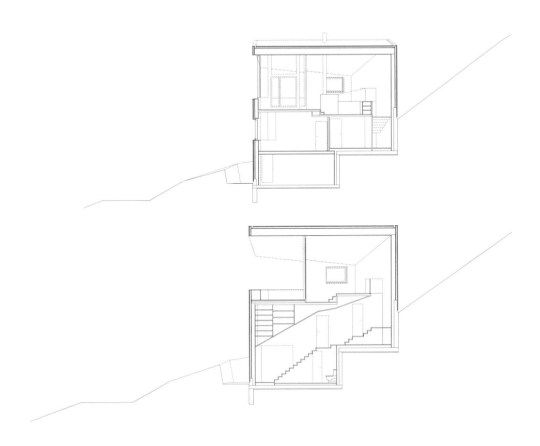

Left: Exterior in winter. Links: Gesamtansicht im Winter. À gauche: Le chalet en hiver. | Right: Sections. Rechts: Schnitte. À droite: Vues en coupe.

Breathtaking views of the surrounding mountain ranges and valleys, and dramatically steep hills characterize the site located in Feldis, Switzerland, 1,500 meters above sea level. The subtle manipulation of a simple timber structure nestled along the contour lines of the hill, anchors this holiday home solidly in its rocky surrounding in a manner akin to a solitary rock outcrop displaced after a rock fall. The seemingly monolithic home appears first narrow and light, then wide and heavy, depending on the perspective viewed.

Eine atemberaubende Aussicht auf die umgebenden Gebirgszüge, Täler und steil aufsteigende Hügel kennzeichnen das Grundstück, 1.500 Meter über dem Meeresspiegel gelegen. Die raffinierte Umgestaltung einer simplen, den Bergkonturen folgenden Holzkonstruktion verankert diese fest in ihrer felsigen Umgebung, ähnlich einem „Ausbiss" nach einem Steinschlag. Das auf den ersten Blick monolithisch wirkende Ferienhaus erscheint einmal schmal und leicht, dann wieder groß und schwer, je nach Perspektive des Betrachters.

Ce chalet construit à flanc de colline à 1500 mètres d'altitude offre des vues panoramiques sur le paysage de montagnes environnant. Il a été développé sur la base d'un édifice préexistant, avec pour résultat une intégration parfaite au paysage. Il s'agit d'une maison de vacances d'aspect monolithique, qui semble fragile et de dimensions réduites au premier abord, mais qui se révèle solide et spacieuse lorsqu'on l'observe de plus près.

Left: Interior. Links: Innenansicht. À gauche: Intérieur. Right: Side view of exterior. Rechts: Seitenansicht. À droite: Vue latérale avec volets ouverts.

From left to right, from above to below:
Exterior, interior, deck, alternative view of interior.
Right: Exterior.

Von links nach rechts, von oben nach unten:
Talansicht, offene Küche, Terrasse, Wohnraum.
Rechts: Gesamtansicht.

De gauche à droite, du haut vers le bas:
Extérieur, intérieur, terrasse, séjour avec cheminée.
À droite: Vue d'ensemble.

EM2N

www.em2n.ch
Client: Gabriela Senti, **Completion:** 2003, **Gross floor area:** 104 m², **Photos:** Hannes Henz Architekturfotograf.

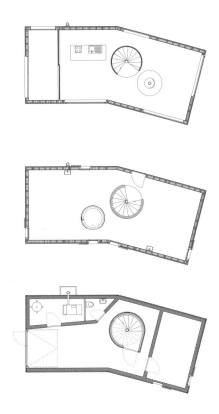

Left: Rear view. Links: Rückansicht. À gauche: Face arrière. | Right: Floor plans. Rechts: Grundrisse. À droite: Plans des différents niveaux.

The construction project intends to reflect the character and qualities of the location. The result is a building that reacts to its location next to an alpine meadow by stretching up to catch the spectacular view on all sides. With the exception of the graveled access way, the alpine meadow is not disrupted around the house. No fence, no landfill, and no excavation changed the setting. On the outside, the house is a variation of the omnipresent chalet theme with its dark wood cladding and small window openings as an image of a chalet tower with huge panoramic windows.

Mit dem Bauvorhaben sollte auf den Charakter und die Qualitäten des Ortes eingegangen werden. Entstanden ist ein Gebäude, das auf die Lage neben einer Alpenwiese reagiert, indem es sich in die Höhe reckt, um auf allen Seiten die spektakuläre Aussicht einzufangen. Rund um das Haus bleibt die Alpenwiese, abgesehen vom gekiesten Zufahrtsweg, ungestört. Kein Zaun, keine Aufschüttung, keine Abgrabung oder Gartengestaltung verändert diesen Ort. Äußerlich variiert das Haus das allgegenwärtige Thema des Chalets mit seiner dunklen Holzverschalung und kleinen Fensteröffnungen zum Bild eines Chaletturms mit riesigen Panoramafenstern.

Les architectes ont conçu ce bâtiment en tenant compte du caractère et de la qualité du site. La hauteur de l'édifice permet aux occupants d'apprécier des vues panoramiques sur les alpages environnants. Ceux-ci sont restés pratiquement intacts : pas de clôture ni de talus ni de fossé ni de jardin, la seule modification apportée consistant ici en une allée de graviers. Le revêtement de façade en bois sombre souligne qu'il s'agit là d'une réinterprétation du thème traditionnel du chalet, la nouveauté résidant dans la silhouette allongée qui évoque une tour, ainsi que dans le percement de grandes fenêtres panoramiques.

Exterior at night. Gesamtansicht bei Dämmerung. Le chalet au crépuscule.

From left to right, from above to below:
Dining area, interior, exterior.
Right: Interior with fireplace.

Von links nach rechts, von oben nach unten:
Essecke, Innenraum, Außenansicht.
Rechts: Wohnraum mit freihängendem Kamin.

De gauche à droite, du haut vers le bas:
Salle à manger, intérieur, extérieur.
À droite: Séjour avec cheminée.

CHESA FALCUN,
KLOSTERS, SWITZERLAND

MARKUS SCHLEGEL

www.descent.co.uk
Client: Private, Completion: 2007, Gross floor area: 480 m², Photos: Albert Zimmermann.

Left: Exterior at dusk. Links: Außenansicht bei Dämmerung. À gauche: Le chalet au crépuscule. | Right: Floor plans. Rechts: Grundrisse. À droite: Plans.

Set over four floors, this imposing chalet has large outdoor terraces and boasts fabulous views across to Gotschna and down the valley to Kublis. Sleeping up to 12 guests, the chalet boasts an impressive master bedroom, as well as a further five spacious ensuite bedrooms, all of which have either a terrace or balcony. To match the outstanding bedrooms are the facilities, which are second to none. They include a sauna, steam shower and massage room, as well as an outdoor hot tub - partially covered.

Auf vier Geschossen bietet dieses weitläufige Chalet großzügige Außenterrassen mit phantastischen Aussichten zum Gotschna und hinunter zum Tal nach Kublis. Platz finden bis zu zwölf Übernachtungsgäste. Das Chalet bietet außer einem beeindruckenden großen Schlafraum fünf weitere geräumige Zimmer mit Bad. Alle verfügen über eine Terrasse oder einen Balkon. Die Ausstattung wird ergänzt durch Sauna, Dampfdusche und Massageraum sowie den teilweise überdachten Außenwhirlpool.

On peut apprécier une vue magnifique qui embrasse le Gotschna et la vallée de Kublis à partir des grandes terrasses de cet imposant chalet sur quatre niveaux. Pouvant abriter douze personnes, le bâtiment dispose d'une chambre de maître particulièrement impressionnante et six autres chambres spacieuses avec salle de bain, terrasse ou balcon. Les équipements de confort sont bien entendu à la hauteur. Citons notamment le sauna, le bain de vapeur, le salon de massage et la baignoire extérieure chauffée partiellement couverte.

From left to right, from above to below:
Bathroom, bedroom, drawing room, bedroom.
Right: Bedroom.

Von links nach rechts, von oben nach unten:
Badezimmer, Schlafzimmer, Salon, Schlafzimmer.
Rechts: Schlafzimmer.

De gauche à droite, du haut vers le bas:
Salle de bain, chambre, salon, autre chambre.
À droite: Baignoire extérieure chauffée.

CHALET REDUX,
LE CHÂBLE, SWITZERLAND

GROUP8 ARCHITECTES ASSOCIÉS

www.group8.ch
Client: Private, **Completion:** 2006, **Gross floor area:** 40 m², **Photos:** DGBP – David Gagnebin-de-Bons and Benoît Pointet.

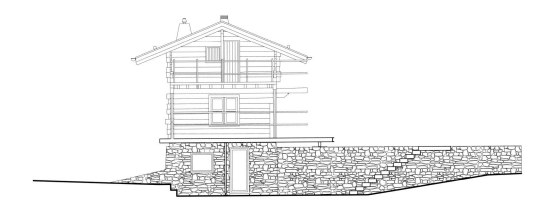

Left: Street side view. Links: Straßenansicht. À gauche: Le chalet vu de la route. | Right: Elevation. Rechts: Ansicht. À droite: Élévation.

The Chalet Redux project is an example of contemporary architecture continuing local traditions in the alpine region. It involves the use of locally available materials and punctual changes that are sensitive and respect the existing structures. A permanent intervention to the architectural design that "has always been there" is fascinating through its landscape context. The entire minimal space renovation was carried out in local larch wood. This resulted in new spaces with minimal space requirements such as the bathroom and bedroom room combination in the English basement.

Das Projekt Chalet Redux ist ein Beispiel für zeitgenössische Architektur in Fortsetzung der einheimischen Traditionen im alpinen Raum. Hierfür stehen der Einsatz lokal vorhandener Materialien, gezielte sowie punktuelle Veränderungen mit Sensibilität und Respekt vor dem Bestand. Eine dauerhafte Intervention für eine „wie schon immer da gewesene Architektur" fasziniert durch den landschaftlichen Kontext. Für die gesamte Renovierung auf Minimalraum wurde das heimische Lärchenholz verwendet. So entstanden neu nutzbare Flächen auf geringstem Raum wie das Zimmer im Sockelgeschoss mit einer Kombination aus Bad und Schlafzimmer.

Ce chalet illustre dans quelle mesure le style alpin traditionnel peut trouver un prolongement dans l'architecture moderne, pour peu que celle-ci sache utiliser les matériaux locaux et apporter des modifications en respectant le bâti antérieur. Situé dans un contexte rural, le chalet Redux donne à merveille l'impression « d'avoir toujours été là ». Et pourtant, il s'agit d'une rénovation réalisée principalement en utilisant du mélèze d'origine locale, afin notamment d'optimiser l'utilisation de l'espace intérieur. C'est ainsi que la pièce du rez-de-chaussée abrite à la fois une chambre et une salle de bain.

From left to right, from above to below:
Front door, staircase, bedroom and bathroom.
Right: Exterior from the front.

Von links nach rechts, von oben nach unten:
Eingangstür, Treppe ins Obergeschoss, Schlaf- und Badezimmer.
Rechts: Eingangsbereich.

De gauche à droite, du haut vers le bas:
Entrée, escalier, chambre/salle de bain.
À droite: Façade principale.

SINGLE-FAMILY HOUSE
LENZ, HINWIL, SWITZERLAND

BEAT ROTHEN DIPL. ARCHITEKT ETH
SIA BSA

www.beatrothen.ch
Client: Private, **Completion:** 2005, **Gross floor area:** 240 m², **Photos:** Gaston Wicky.

Left: Exterior. Links: Gesamtansicht. À gauche: Façade. | Right: Secction. Rechts: Schnitt. À droite: Vue en coupe.

This crimson object in the densely constructed single-family district of "Im Lenz" resembles a sculpture that has been retroactively placed in a garden. The building structure resembles a temporarily constructed tent, distinguishing itself from the surrounding, mostly traditional homes. The structure was reduced to projecting concrete plates and a few load-bearing walls. The resulting concrete frame constitutes the thermal mass of the building and is heated in winter. A thermally insulated lightweight construction is placed on this frame. Its untreated OSB plates characterize the style of the building's interior design.

Wie eine Skulptur, die zur Zierde nachträglich in einen Garten gestellt wurde, wirkt dieses karminrote Objekt im dichten, fertig gebauten Einfamilienhausquartier „Im Lenz". Die Gebäudestruktur erinnert an ein temporär aufgebautes Zelt und hebt sich damit von den umliegenden, meist konventionellen Häusern ab. Die Struktur wurde auf auskragende Betonplatten und wenige tragende Wände reduziert. Das daraus entstehende Betongerippe bildet die Speichermasse des Gebäudes und wird im Winter beheizt. Über dieses Gerippe ist eine wärmegedämmte Leichtbaukonstruktion gestülpt, die mit ihren rohen OSB-Platten den innenarchitektonischen Ausdruck des Gebäudes bestimmt.

Construit dans un quartier de pavillons préfabriqués, ce bâtiment rouge carmin ressemble à une sculpture décorative posée a posteriori dans un jardin. De plus, son aspect général qui évoque une tente ou un édifice temporaire le distingue par rapport aux bâtiments conventionnels qui l'entourent. Il s'agit d'une structure réduite à des plaques en béton et quelques murs porteurs, le béton permettant d'accumuler la chaleur en hiver. Le reste de l'enveloppe se compose de panneaux OSB isolés à l'extérieur et laissés bruts à l'intérieur, ce qui donne aux pièces une atmosphère particulière et caractéristique.

Left: Living area. Links: Wohnbereich. À gauche: Séjour. Right: Hallway, interior. Rechts: Flur und Badewanne, Obergeschoss. À droite: Couloir, vue de l'intérieur.

From left to right, from above to below:
Exterior, living area, interior, hallway.
Right: Exterior from roadside.

Von links nach rechts, von oben nach unten:
Seitenansicht, Wohnbereich, Interieur, Flur.
Rechts: Gesamtansicht.

De gauche à droite, du haut vers le bas:
Extérieur, séjour, intérieur, couloir.
À droite: Le chalet vu de la route.

NEW BUILDING IN SCAIANO,
SCAIANO, SWITZERLAND

MARKUS WESPI JÉRÔME DE MEURON ARCHITEKTEN BSA

www.wespidemeuron.ch
Client: Private, **Completion:** 2004, **Gross floor area:** 70 m², **Photos:** Hannes Henz, Architekturfotograf.

Left: Exterior with patio and lake view. Links: Außenansicht mit Terrasse und Seeblick. À gauche: maison, lac et montagne. | Right: Elevation. Rechts: Ansicht. À droite: Élévation.

The reconstructed ruin of a stable is located in a prominent position at the edge of the village where it interacts with the village and the landscape. New interventions were not obviously and blatantly placed in contrast to the old substance, instead a contemporary clarity was extracted from the historical substance. By removing the old pitched roof and reduction of the structure to a simple cube, the existing contours were made visible. An additionally required increase in volume for a bathroom is implemented on the mountainside underneath the terrain where it does not affect the cubic structure and proportions.

Die umgebaute Stallruine befindet sich an markanter Lage am Dorfrand und steht sowohl im Dialog zum Dorf wie auch zur Landschaft. Neue Eingriffe werden nicht augenfällig und kontrastreich der alten Substanz gegenübergestellt, vielmehr wird eine zeitgemäße Klarheit aus der historischen Substanz herausgeschält. Durch die Entfernung des alten Satteldaches und Reduktion des Baukörpers zu einem einfachen Kubus werden seine vorhandenen Konturen sichtbar gemacht. Um Kubatur und Proportion nicht zu beeinträchtigen, wird eine zusätzlich nötige Volumenvergrößerung für ein Bad bergseitig unter Terrain realisiert.

Cette ancienne écurie se dresse sur un promontoire en bordure d'un village, pour ainsi dire à l'interface entre la nature et l'architecture. La rénovation a été conduite en respectant la structure d'origine, tout en y introduisant les lignes claires typiques du style contemporain. Le toit à deux pentes a été remplacé par une dalle, le bâtiment prenant ainsi une forme presque cubique, c'est-à-dire résolument moderne. Afin de conserver les proportions d'origine tout en augmentant la surface habitable, les architectes ont construit la salle de bain en décaissement au niveau du sous-sol.

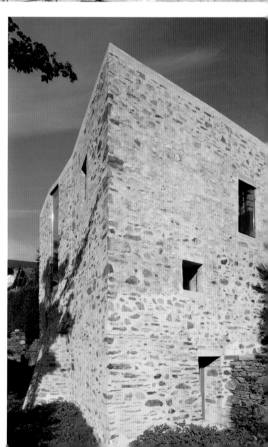

From left to right, from above to below:
Dining area, patio, kitchen, exterior view.
Right: Living area with fireplace.

Von links nach rechts, von oben nach unten:
Essecke, Terrasse, Küche, Außenansicht.
Rechts: Wohnzimmer mit Kamin.

De gauche à droite, du haut vers le bas:
Salle à manger, terrasse, cuisine, extérieur.
À droite: Séjour avec cheminée.

CHESA LUMPAZ,
ST. MORITZ, SWITZERLAND

ARCHITECT: NICO RENSCH
IN COLLABORATION WITH
VALENTIN BEARTH
PROJECT MANAGEMENT AND
INTERIOR SOLUTIONS: MAUNALEJ

www.architeam.co.uk, www.maunalej.com
Client: Private, **Completion:** 2007, **Gross floor area:** 900 m², **Photos:** Courtesy of Leo Trippi.

Left: Living room with fireplace. Links: Wohnzimmer mit Kamin. À gauche: Séjour avec cheminée. | Right: Ground floor plan. Rechts: Grundriss Erdgeschoss. À droite: Plan du rez-de-chaussée.

Chesa Lumpaz is a modern, contemporary and luxurious 900 square meter villa, set on five floors connected by stairs as well as an elevator. It features the most modern systems in home comfort, entertainment, spa and wellness. With a professional full-time service team and a private five-star chef. It has four large double bedrooms, each with en-suite bath/shower rooms. Adjacent to the two double bedrooms on level two, is a children's master bedroom, including a large double bed, bath, shower and a separate smaller bedroom for a nanny. Chesa Lumpaz offers modern amenities and the highest standards of luxury.

Chesa Lumpaz ist eine zeitgemäße und luxuriöse Villa von 900 Quadratmetern. Ihre fünf Geschosse werden von Treppen und einem Aufzug miteinander verbunden. Sie verfügt über den modernsten Wohnkomfort, beste Unterhaltungsmöglichkeiten sowie Spa- und Wellnessbereich. Die vier Doppelzimmer sind mit eigenen Bädern/Duschräumen ausgestattet. An die beiden Doppelzimmer in der zweiten Etage grenzt ein Schlafraum für Kinder, der ein Doppelbett, Bad, Dusche und einen separaten Bereich für ein Kindermädchen enthält. Das Haus bietet moderne Annehmlichkeiten und Luxus auf höchstem Niveau.

Cette villa moderne de grand luxe offre une surface habitable de neuf cents mètres carrés répartis sur cinq niveaux desservis par un escalier et un ascenseur. On y trouve le dernier cri de la technique, tant en matière de confort ménager que d'équipements de loisirs ou de bien-être. Un chef cuisinier cinq étoiles et du personnel de maison professionnel sont constamment à la disposition des occupants, qui logent dans quatre grandes chambres avec salle de bain. Celles du niveau deux se complètent d'une chambre d'enfants avec salle de bain et chambre de bonne séparée. La villa Chesa Lumpaz offre ainsi tout le confort moderne et satisfait aux plus hautes exigences en matière de luxe.

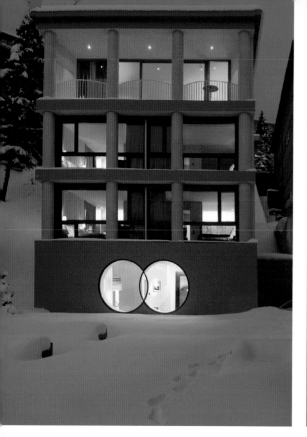

From left to right, from above to below:
Front façade at night, hallway, wellness area, entrance.
Right: View to bedroom from bathroom.

Von links nach rechts, von oben nach unten:
Vorderfassade bei Nacht, Flur, Wellnessbereich, Eingangsbereich.
Rechts: Blick vom Bade- zum Schlafzimmer.

De gauche à droite, du haut vers le bas:
Le chalet la nuit, couloir, espace wellness, entrée.
À droite: La chambre vue de la salle de bains.

VILLA B.,
ST. LÉONARD, SWITZERLAND

GROUP8 ARCHITECTES ASSOCIÉS

www.group8.ch
Client: Private, **Completion:** 2005, **Gross floor area:** 213 m², **Photos:** DGBP – David Gagnebin-de-Bons and Benoît Pointet.

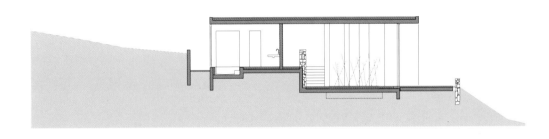

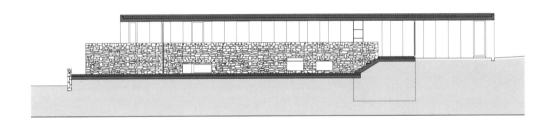

Left: Exterior view with surrounding countryside. Links: Terrasse mit Aussicht. À gauche: Terrasse et vignoble. | Right: Sections. Rechts: Schnitte. À droite: Vues en coupe.

"Residing in a vineyard" is the basic concept for the residential home in St. Léonard. The key architectural themes are horizontality, mineralogy, and integration into the surrounding landscape. A vineyard wall serves as a structural element of the living room, dividing it into two half levels. Exposed concrete walls protect the upper level for the private rooms, while the lower generous level for the common rooms opens up to the landscape with a large glass façade. These rooms and several terraces allow various uses of the outdoor space in interaction with the landscape.

„Einen Weinberg bewohnen" ist das Ausgangsmotiv für dieses Wohnhaus in St. Léonard. Horizontalität, Mineralität, Integration in die umgebende Landschaft sind die Leitideen der architektonischen Reflexion. Eine Mauer des Weinbergs dient als strukturelles Element des Wohnraums und gliedert diesen in zwei halbe Niveaus. Die obere Ebene für die privaten Räume ist durch Sichtbetonwände geschützt, während sich die untere, großzügige Ebene für die Gemeinschaftsräume mit einer großen Glasfassade zur Landschaft öffnet. Diese Räume und mehrere Terrassen erlauben eine unterschiedliche Nutzung des Außenraums im Dialog mit der Landschaft.

Les architectes ont conçu ce bâtiment autour de trois axes (horizontalité, minéralité et intégration au paysage), ceci afin de concrétiser une ambition claire : habiter au cœur d'un vignoble. Le mur de soutènement d'une ancienne terrasse structure l'espace habitable selon deux niveaux. Un mur en béton but de coffrage protège les pièces privées du niveau supérieur, tandis que le séjour du niveau inférieur s'ouvre sur le paysage grâce à une cloison entièrement vitrée. La maison se complète de plusieurs terrasses aux fonctions diverses qui assurent un dialogue entre nature et architecture.

From left to right, from above to below:
Stone fireplace, detail of fireplace, view into interior from exterior.
Right: Exterior and surrounding landscape.

Von links nach rechts, von oben nach unten:
Steinkamin, Detail, Glasfassade.
Rechts: Einbettung in die Landschaft.

De gauche à droite, du haut vers le bas:
Cheminée en pierre, détail de cheminée,
intérieur vu au travers de la baie vitrée.
À droite: Maison dans les vignes.

K_M.ARCHITEKTUR DI DANIEL SAUTER

www.k-m-architektur.com

Client: Private, **Completion:** 2007, **Gross floor area:** 140 m², **Photos:** Courtesy of k_m.architektur DI Daniel Sauter.

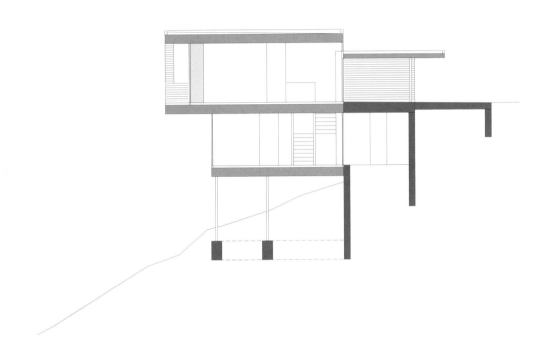

Left: Exterior view from below. Links: Talansicht. À gauche: Vue d'ensemble. | Right: Section. Rechts: Schnitt. À droite: Vue en coupe.

The functionally designed two-floor residential home is located in a rural area on a property with a view of Lake Walen and the opposite shore. The aim of the project was to create a building with an ecological, cost-effective and high-quality architecture, whose exterior appearance and materials harmoniously fit into the surrounding agricultural landscape. Equipped with triple glazed thermal protection windows, the building is heated exclusively with wood. The structure, windows, façade and floor covers of the building consist of untreated local larch wood.

Das funktionell gestaltete, zweigeschossige Wohnhaus steht in ländlicher Gegend auf einem Grundstück mit Blick auf den Walensee und das gegenüberliegende Ufer. Ziel der Bauaufgabe war es, eine ökologische, kostengünstige und qualitativ hochwertige Architektur zu schaffen, welche sich durch äußere Erscheinung und Materialität harmonisch in die landwirtschaftlich geprägte Umgebung einfügt. Das mit dreifach verglasten Wärmeschutzfenstern ausgestattete Gebäude wird ausschließlich über Holzfeuerung beheizt. Die Konstruktion, Fenster, Fassade und Bodenbeläge des Gebäudes bestehen aus naturbelassenem, einheimischem Lärchenholz.

En construisant cette maison de campagne fonctionnelle sur deux niveaux avec vue directe sur le lac de Walen, les architectes ont cherché à réaliser un édifice écologique de haute qualité, tout en minimisant à la fois les coûts et l'impact sur l'environnement. Les fenêtres sont en triple vitrage et le chauffage assuré exclusivement par un poêle à bois. Pour les murs porteurs, les fenêtres, les planchers et le revêtement de façade, les architectes ont choisi du bois de mélèze non traité d'origine locale.

Left: Deck with view to the lake, interior, bedroom and deck. Links: Terrasse mit Seeblick, Interieur, Schlafzimmer. À gauche: Vue de la terrasse et du lac, intérieur, chambre.

Right: Living room with fireplace. Rechts: Wohnbereich mit Kamin. À droite: Séjour avec cheminée.

From left to right, from above to below:
Exterior with lawn, dining room with lake view, exterior view.
Right: Garage entrance.

Von links nach rechts, von oben nach unten:
Gesamtansicht, Essecke, Vorderansicht.
Rechts: Eingangsansicht.

De gauche à droite, du haut vers le bas:
Maison et prairie, salle à manger avec vue sur le lac,
maison au crépuscule.
À droite: Entrée.

CHALET PIERRE AVOI,
VERBIER, SWITZERLAND

ARCHITECTS: STEPHAN LUISIER AND
OLIVIER FILIEZ. DESIGNER: MIRA
ZOSMER

www.descent.co.uk

Client: Private, **Completion:** 2008, **Gross floor area:** 450 m², **Photos:** Joe Condron.

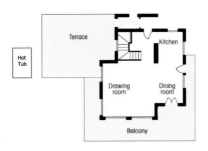

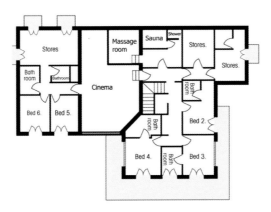

Left: General view. Links: Gesamtansicht. À gauche: Vue d'ensemble. | Right: Ground floor and lower floor plans. Rechts: Grundriss Erdgeschoss und Untergeschoss. À droite: Plans du rez-de-chaussée et du sous-sol.

Located in the secluded Plan-Praz area of Verbier lies Pierre Avoi; a chalet that has mastered the juxtaposition of comfort and style within breathtaking surroundings. The chalet sleeps 12 guests in six bedrooms. The interior has been lovingly designed by the owner using natural mineral walls and striking pieces of art. The open plan living area features a roaring fireplace and floor to ceiling picture windows. The west side of the chalet boasts uninterrupted views of endless snowy fields, which can be enjoyed from the Jacuzzi, or from the large decked terrace.

Das Chalet Pierre Avoi liegt in Verbiers abgeschiedenem Gebiet Plan-Praz. Es präsentiert in einer atemberaubenden Umgebung ein gelungenes Nebeneinander von Komfort und Stil. Im Chalet können zwölf Gäste in sechs Zimmern übernachten. Die Innenräume wurden vom Eigentümer mit Wänden aus natürlichen Mineralien und Kunstwerken liebevoll gestaltet. In den Wohnbereichen mit offenem Grundriss finden sich Kamine und deckenhohe Panoramafenster. An der Westseite des Chalets kann man vom Whirlpool oder von der großzügigen Terrasse aus einen freien Blick auf endlose Schneefelder genießen.

Situé à Verbier, au lieu-dit Plan-Praz, c'est-à-dire dans un site magnifique, ce chalet associe à merveille le confort et le grand style. On y trouve six chambres pour deux personnes. La décoration intérieure se caractérise par l'usage de la pierre naturelle, rehaussée par des œuvres d'art exposées avec goût. Le vaste séjour présente une grande cheminée et des murs entièrement vitrés. Les immenses champs de neige qui s'étendent aux alentours sont visibles de la terrasse partiellement couverte et de toutes les fenêtres, notamment celles de la salle de bain avec jacuzzi.

From left to right, from above to below:
Drawing room with fireplace, interior view, bedroom.
Right: View at night.

Von links nach rechts, von oben nach unten:
Salon mit Kamin, Innenansicht, Schlafzimmer.
Rechts: Nachtansicht.

De gauche à droite, du haut vers le bas:
Séjour avec cheminée, intérieur, chambre.
À droite: Le chalet au crépuscule.

WOODEN CABIN,
VOLLÈGES, SWITZERLAND

GROUP8 ARCHITECTES ASSOCIÉS

www.group8.ch

Client: Private, **Completion:** 2005, **Gross floor area:** 250 m², **Photos:** DGBP – David Gagnebin-de-Bons and Benoît Pointet.

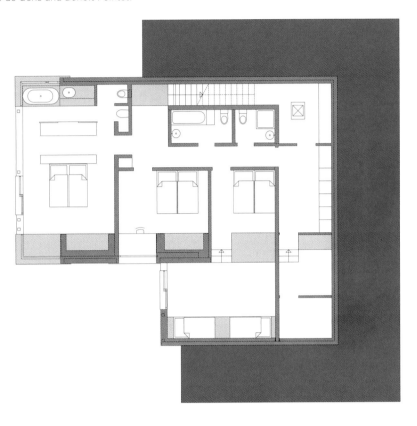

Left: Wooden façade. Links: Holzfassade. À gauche: Façade en bois. | Right: Ground floor plan. Rechts: Grundriss Erdgeschoss. À droite: Plan du rez-de-chaussée.

The Wooden Cabin project in Vollèges suggests a new interpretation of the traditional alpine chalet elements. The materials of the building provide the object with its unique characteristics while highlighting its firm connection to the ground. A roof made of limestone plates, traditional to the Wallis region, rests on two over dimensional thick longitudinal walls. The integration of the functional areas in the double structure makes them habitable. The walls are constructed of horizontal thin layers of larch wood, which are mounted on a frame construction, each slightly horizontally displaced from the next one.

Das Projekt Wooden Cabin in Vollèges schlägt eine Neuinterpretation der traditionellen Elemente alpiner Chalets vor. Die Materialität des Gebäudes gibt dem Objekt seine Charaktereigenschaften und unterstreicht seine Verankerung im Boden. Ein Dach aus Kalksteinplatten, wie es traditionell im Wallis gebaut wird, liegt auf zwei überdimensional dicken Längswänden. Aufgrund der Integration der Nutzbereiche in die Doppelung der Wände können diese bewohnt werden. Der Wandaufbau setzt sich aus horizontalen, dünnen Lagen von Lärchenholz zusammen, welche mit einer jeweils leichten horizontalen Verschiebung zur nächsten Schicht auf einer Unterkonstruktion montiert sind.

Ce chalet construit à Vollèges, dans le canton du Valais, réinterprète le style alpin traditionnel. L'usage quasi exclusif du bois caractérise l'ensemble et enracine le bâtiment dans son environnement. Le toit en lauzes calcaires, typique de la région, repose sur deux murs d'appuis surdimensionnés qui intègrent certains éléments fonctionnels afin d'optimiser l'utilisation de l'espace. Le revêtement intérieur et extérieur a été réalisé en fines planches de mélèze disposées horizontalement de part et d'autre d'une structure médiane.

From left to right, from above to below:
Bathroom, stairs, exterior, alternative view of exterior.
Right: Window seats.

Von links nach rechts, von oben nach unten:
Badzimmer, Treppe, Küchenfenster, Fassadendetail.
Rechts: Sitzecke.

De gauche à droite, du haut vers le bas:
Salle de bain, escalier, deux vues de l'extérieur.
À droite: Bancs près de la fenêtre.

CHALET GRACE,
ZERMATT, SWITZERLAND

PETER PERREN AND SARAH
NEWMAN

www.descent.co.uk
Client: Sarah Newman, Completion: 2009, Gross floor area: 650 m², Photos: Jan Baldwin.

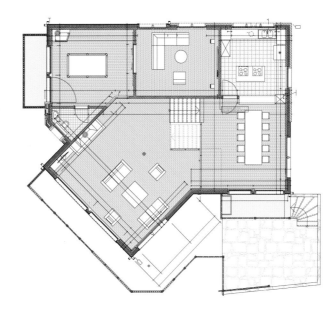

Left: Living space. Links: Wohnraum. À gauche: Séjour. | Right: Floor plan. Rechts: Grundriss. À droite: Plan.

Chalet Grace sits in a prime location, in the exclusive Petit Village with breathtaking views of the Matterhorn. Built to an exquisite finish, Grace features double-height floor to ceiling windows on all three levels and a dramatic beamed interior. It has numerous south-facing balconies capturing the inspiring mountain views. Accommodation is luxurious, spacious and light, offering five ensuite double or twin bedrooms. It also boasts a luxuriously-seated home cinema, a games room with a pool table, a spacious glass fronted wellness center including a sauna, shower room, massage room, pilates/yoga space, outdoor hot tub and shower.

Chalet Grace, in bester Lage im exklusiven Petit Village gelegen, bietet eine atemberaubende Sicht auf das Matterhorn. Charakteristisch sind eine exquisite Bauausführung, zweigeschossige Fenster auf allen drei Ebenen und ein spektakuläres Gebälk im Innern. Zahlreiche Südbalkone fangen die begeisternde Sicht auf die Berge ein. Die Unterbringung ist luxuriös, großzügig und hell. Zur Verfügung stehen fünf Doppelzimmer mit Bad. Es bietet außerdem ein luxuriös bestuhltes Heimkino, einen Spielraum mit einem Billardtisch und einen großzügigen, verglasten Wellnessbereich mit Sauna, Dusch- und Massageraum, Pilates-/Yoga-Bereiche sowie einen Außenwhirlpool mit Dusche.

Le chalet Grace, situé dans le « Petit Village » de Zermatt (une copropriété de grand luxe), offre une vue privilégiée sur le mont Cervin. L'intérieur, aménagé avec goût, présente à tous les étages des poutres apparentes et des pans de murs entièrement vitrés. Plusieurs balcons situés au sud font face à un paysage de montagne particulièrement inspirant. On y trouve cinq chambres pour deux personnes spacieuses, luxueuses et claires, ainsi qu'une salle de projection, une salle de jeux avec billard et un espace wellness avec sauna, douche, salon de massage, salle de yoga et baignoire extérieure chauffée.

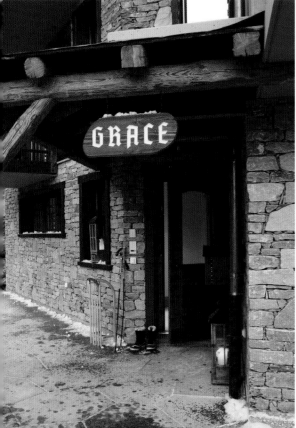
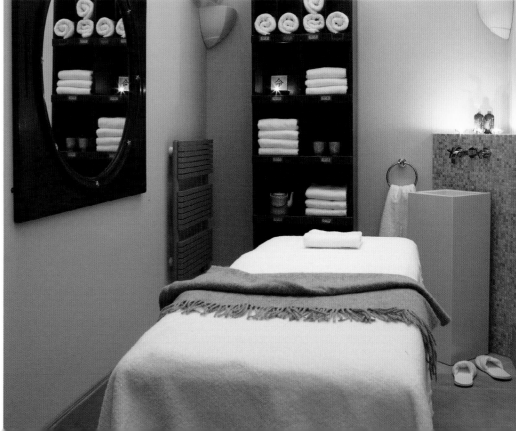

From left to right, from above to below:
Bathroom, wellness area, entrance view, spa area.
Right: Bedroom.

Von links nach rechts, von oben nach unten:
Badezimmer, Wellnessbereich, Eingangsansicht, Spa-Bereich.
Rechts: Schlafzimmer.

De gauche à droite, du haut vers le bas:
Salle de bain, espace wellness, entrée, spa.
À droite: Chambre.

CHALET MAURICE,
ZERMATT, SWITZERLAND

PETER PERREN AND MAGALI DE TSCHARNER

www.descent.co.uk

Client: Private, **Completion:** 2008, **Gross floor area:** 350 m², **Photos:** Jan Baldwin (260, 262 b. l., 263), Jeremy Wilson.

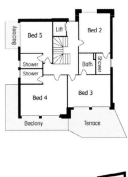

Left: Bedroom with open fireplace. Links: Schlafzimmer mit offenem Kamin. À gauche: Chambre avec cheminée. | Right: Floor plans. Rechts: Grundrisse. À droite: Plans.

The interior, transformed by renowned designer Magali von Tscharner, parades sumptuous fabrics and rich wood in palates of charcoal grey, cream and white, all combining to form a luxurious and chic alpine retreat. Large south-facing balconies extend from each floor, offering the perfect spot to recline and survey the breathtaking views of the Matterhorn. The modern interior is complemented by all the essential facilities needed to revitalise spirits: massage room, sauna, and outdoor hot tub; to ensure no unnecessary energy is used when off the slopes, a funicular lift provides access to the chalet.

Das von der Designerin Magali von Tscharner umgestaltete Innere präsentiert kostbare Stoffe und prachtvolles Holz in dunkelgrauen, cremefarbenen und weißen Ausführungen. Das Interieur bildet ein luxuriöses und elegantes Refugium in den Bergen. Große Südbalkone vor jedem Geschoss sind der ideale Ort zum Ausspannen und Betrachten der Aussichten auf das Matterhorn. Ergänzt wird der moderne Innenbereich durch einen Spa-Bereich mit Massageraum, Sauna und Außenwhirlpool. Eine weitere Besonderheit ist der Schrägaufzug über den das Chalet erschlossen werden kann.

Les aménagements intérieurs, œuvre de la décoratrice Magali von Tscharner, associent de sompteux tissus et des tons de bois gris, crème et blanc pour former un refuge alpin luxueux et chic. À chaque étage, des balcons orientés au sud invitent à se reposer en appréciant des vues magnifiques sur le mont Cervin. La décoration moderne se complète de tous les équipements nécessaires à se ressourcer : sauna, salon de massage et baignoire extérieure chauffée. L'accès au chalet se fait par funiculaire.

From left to right, from above to below:
Living space, detail exterior, bathroom, bedroom.
Right: Drawing room.

Von links nach rechts, von oben nach unten:
Wohnraum, Außendetail, Badezimmer, Schlafzimmer.
Rechts: Salon.

De gauche à droite, du haut vers le bas:
Séjour, détail de la façade, salle de bain, chambre.
À droite: Salon.

SPIRAL HOUSE PIGNIU,
ZURICH, SWITZERLAND

www.dgj.ch
Client: Private, **Completion:** 2004, **Gross floor area:** 150 m², **Photos:** Ralph Feiner.

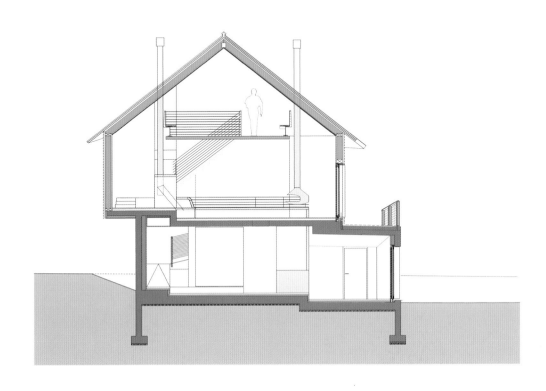

Left: General view. Links: Gesamtansicht. À gauche: Vue d'ensemble. | **Right:** Section. Rechts: Schnitt. À droite: Vue en coupe.

The spaces of this week-end house are connected in a spiral movement, divided by different levels. The outside wall is wrapped around twice, like a continuous skin, the lower part is kept in concrete with a flat modular formwork – the upper one is of prefabricated wooden elements, covered with hand-cut larch shingles. The larch windows and shutters are the same for both levels – accentuating the continuity of the band. The house's appearance is integrating with the village and the rough mountainous environment. The inner spaces are open and light, they dynamically connect the inhabitants with the landscape views.

Die in verschiedene Ebenen aufgeteilten Bereiche dieses Wochenendhauses sind in einer spiralartigen Bewegung miteinander verbunden. Die Außenmauer wickelt sich wie eine durchgehende Haut doppelt um das Gebäude. Die untere Ebene besteht aus Beton in flachen Modul-Schalungen, die obere wurde aus vorgefertigten Holzelementen hergestellt und mit handgefertigten Lärchenholzschindeln gedeckt. Durch die gleichen Lärchenholz-Fenster und -Klappläden in beiden Geschossen wird die Kontinuität des Gebäudes akzentuiert. Das Äußere des Hauses passt sich seiner dörflichen Umgebung und der umliegenden Gebirgslandschaft an. Die Innenräume sind hell und offen und verbinden die Bewohner somit auf dynamische Weise mit der Natur.

Une spirale relie les différents niveaux et espaces de cette maison de week-end. Le rez-de-chaussée se compose de béton coulé en coffrage modulaire, tandis que les étages supérieurs sont pourvus d'un double revêtement composé de panneaux de bois préfabriqués et de bardeaux en mélèze taillés à la main, l'ensemble formant une enveloppe continue. La présence des mêmes fenêtres et persiennes en mélèze à tous les niveaux contribue à l'unification des façades. Ce chalet, parfaitement intégré au village et à la montagne environnante, présente un intérieur lumineux et de plan ouvert qui offre des vues magnifiques sur le paysage.

Exterior at night. Außenansicht bei Nacht. La maison au crépuscule.

From left to right, from above to below:
Bathroom, bedroom, living area, dining room.
Right: Upstairs.

Von links nach rechts, von oben nach unten:
Badezimmer, Schlafzimmer, Wohnzimmer mit
hängendem Kamin, Essecke.
Rechts: Wohnbereich im Obergeschoss.

De gauche à droite, du haut vers le bas:
Salle de bain, chambre, séjour, salle à manger.
À droite: Vue du niveau supérieur.

KENT CHALET,
WHITSTABLE, UNITED KINGDOM

STUDIOMAMA

www.studiomama.com
Client: Nina Tolstrup, Jack Mama, **Completion:** 2007, **Gross floor area:** 33 m², **Photos:** Gitte Stærbo.

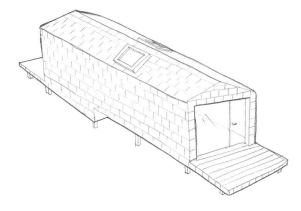

Left: Interior with ocean view. Links: Interieur mit Meerblick. À gauche: Séjour avec vue sur la mer. | Right: Sketch. Rechts: Skizze. À droite: Esquisse.

The beach chalet pared down to the essentials: eat, drink, sleep, and view. London-based Danish designer Nina Tolstrup of Studiomama wanted a weekend retreat to escape life in Shoreditch, so she bought a small plot of land on the shore in Whitstable, a seaside town located in northeast Kent. The 36 square meter structure is located in the middle of a row of 25 tiny cottages, sits on galvanized steel stilts, and is clad with cedar shingles. The interior is sawn softwood; and the focus is the sea view. A sleeping loft accommodates Tolstrup and her husband, and her two children sleep in bunks.

Das Strandhaus ist auf das Wesentliche reduziert: Essen, Trinken, Schlafen und den Ausblick genießen. Die in London ansässige dänische Designerin Nina Tolstrup von Studiomama wünschte sich ein Wochenendhaus. Für die Realisierung erwarb sie eine kleine Parzelle an der Küste von Whitstable, einer Stadt nordöstlich von Kent. Die 36 Quadratmeter große Konstruktion inmitten einer Reihe von 25 winzigen Häusern ist auf verzinkte Stahlstelzen gesetzt und mit Zedernholz eingeschindelt. Innen besteht die Verkleidung aus Nadelschnittholz. Das Hauptaugenmerk liegt auf dem Meerblick. Als Schlafzimmer nutzt das Ehepaar einen Schlafboden, während die beiden Kinder in eingebauten Betten schlafen.

La styliste danoise Nina Tolstrup, qui travaille à Londres, souhaitait disposer d'un pied-à-terre au bord de la mer. Elle a donc acheté un terrain de trente-six mètres carrés sur la plage de Whitstable, sur la côte nord-ouest du Kent, à un endroit déjà occupé par vingt-cinq pavillons de plage, et y a construit son propre pavillon, pourvu de l'essentiel, à savoir une cuisine, une chambre et une vue directe sur la mer. L'édifice repose sur des poutres en acier galvanisé et est recouvert de shingles en bois de cèdre. Les aménagements intérieurs sont également en bois, à l'exception du pignon face à la mer, qui est entièrement vitré. On trouve à l'intérieur une mezzanine pour les parents et un lit gigogne pour les enfants.

Left: Open kitchen. Links: Offene Küche. À gauche: Cuisine. Right: Entry way. Rechts: Terrasse. À droite: Terrasse et entrée côté rue.

From left to right, from above to below:
Living area, view from loft, bedroom, stove.
Right: Exterior with porch.

Von links nach rechts, von oben nach unten:
Blick in den Wohnraum, Meerblick, Schlafbereich, Kamin.
Rechts: Gesamtansicht.

De gauche à droite, du haut vers le bas:
Séjour, vue de la mezzanine vers le séjour, mezzanine avec
fenêtre panoramique, poêle à bois.
À droite: Terrasse côté plage.

EMIGRATION CANYON RESIDENCE,
EMIGRATION CANYON, UT, USA

SPARANO + MOONEY
ARCHITECTURE

www.sparanomooney.com

Client: John P. Sparano & Anne G. Mooney, **Completion:** 2009, **Gross floor area:** 232 m², **Photos:** SMA.

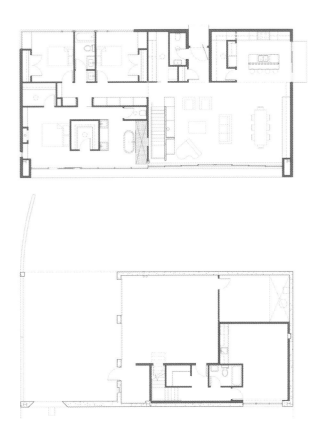

Left: Exterior with façade detail. Links: Fassadendetail. À gauche: Extérieur avec le détail de façade. | Right: Floor plans. Rechts: Grundrisse. À droite: Plans.

Located in Emigration Canyon just above Salt Lake City, Utah, this single-family residence of 232 square meters was designed for a couple with young children. The home was designed to capture expansive canyon views while offering a series of gathering and entertainment spaces for the family, both indoors and outside. The great room opens to the canyon with a nine-meter operable wall to transform the space into an outdoor room. The warm colors of corten steel cladding combine with a board-formed wood textured concrete and glass for a contextual, low-maintenance and modern material palette.

Dieses 232 Quadratmeter große Einfamilienhaus im Emigration Canyon oberhalb von Salt Lake City in Utah wurde für ein Ehepaar mit kleinen Kindern geplant. Es soll den weiten Blick auf den Canyon einfangen und der Familie innen wie außen eine Reihe von Räumen für das gesellige Beisammensein bieten. Das weitläufige Zimmer öffnet sich zum Canyon mit einer neun Meter breiten mobilen Trennwand, die den Innenbereich zu einem Außenraum macht. Die warmen Farben der Verkleidung aus Corten-Stahl ergeben zusammen mit dem Schalbrettmuster des Betons und dem Glas eine homogene, pflegeleichte und moderne Materialpalette.

Cette maison construite sur les hauteurs qui dominent Salt Lake City, dans l'Utah, dispose d'une surface habitable de 232 mètres carrés et abrite un jeune couple avec enfants. Elle offre des vues remarquables sur les environs et inclut des espaces de réunion tant à l'intérieur qu'à l'extérieur. Citons notamment la grande pièce dont le mur de neuf mètres de long est pourvu de panneaux de verre coulissants, de sorte que cet espace s'ouvre entièrement sur le paysage alentour. L'enveloppe, qui associe le verre, les plaques d'acier Corten et le béton coulé dans des planches en bois naturel, est d'un aspect moderne et ne requiert que peu d'entretien.

From left to right, from above to below:
Exterior at night, dining room, exterior.
Right: Exterior with mountains.

Von links nach rechts, von oben nach unten:
Talansicht bei Nacht, Wohn- und Esszimmer, Gesamtansicht.
Rechts: Eingangsansicht.

De gauche à droite, du haut vers le bas:
La maison la nuit, salle à manger, extérieur.
À droite: La maison dans son environnement.

NEAL CREEK RESIDENCE,
HOOD RIVER, OR, USA

PAUL MCKEAN ARCHITECTURE

www.pmckean.com

Client: Paul McKean, Amy Donohue, **Completion:** 2007, **Gross floor area:** 87 m², **Photos:** Paul Mckean.

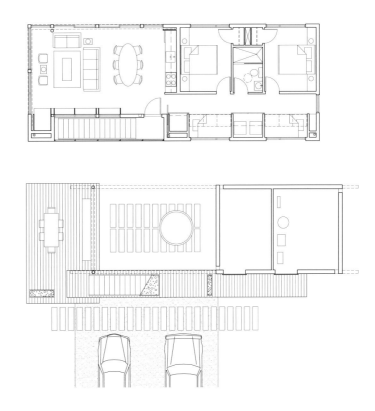

Left: Exterior view through snowy trees. Links: Außenansicht im Winter. À gauche: Le chalet en hiver. | Right: Floor plans. Rechts: Grundrisse. À droite: Plans des différents niveaux.

The Neal Creek Residence treads lightly upon its surroundings, maximizing valley and water views with minimal impact to the natural environment. The owners - windsurfing and snowboarding enthusiasts were interested in a modest home that would be highly efficient and ecologically minded. Their wooded two-acre parcel of land presented many unique challenges including wetlands, creek protection setbacks, and floodplain restrictions. The design solution for the two-bedroom house addresses these issues by elevating the habitable space one full floor above grade. Views to the creek are enhanced from this position and the living spaces float within the treetops.

Das Wohnhaus hinterlässt kaum Spuren an seinem Standort. Die Aussichten auf das Tal und das Wasser werden mit minimalen Eingriffen in die natürliche Umgebung maximiert. Den Eigentümern, begeisterten Windsurfern und Snowboardern, lag an einer bescheidenen Unterkunft, die effizient und umweltfreundlich sein sollte. Das bewaldete, 8.000 Quadratmeter große Areal bereitete wegen der Feuchtgebiete, der vorgeschriebenen Schutzabstände für den Bach und der Einschränkungen für Auen viele Probleme. Der Entwurf löst die Aufgabe, indem der bewohnbare Raum um ein Vollgeschoss über das Bodenniveau angehoben wird. Dadurch ist der kleine Fluss besser sichtbar, und die Wohnräume schweben in den Baumkronen.

Pour cette maison avec deux chambres, les architectes se sont efforcés de minimiser l'impact sur l'environnement, tout en optimisant les vues sur la vallée et la rivière qui passe à proximité. Les propriétaires (qui aiment pratiquer la planche à neige) souhaitaient une maison simple, efficace et écologique. Le terrain boisé d'un peu moins d'un hectare dont ils disposaient présentait de nombreuses contraintes, liées à la présence de la rivière et de la plaine inondable qui la borde. C'est pourquoi le bâtiment a été construit sur pilotis. Cette position surélevée place les espaces habitables au niveau de la cime des arbres et offre des vues panoramiques sur la nature environnante.

From left to right, from above to below:
Detail façade, exterior, living area with open kitchen.
Right: Exterior during spring.

Von links nach rechts, von oben nach unten:
Fassadendetail, Außenansicht, Wohnbereich mit offeneer Küche
Rechts: Gesamtansicht im Frühling.

De gauche à droite, du haut vers le bas:
Détail de la façade, le chalet dans son environnement,
cuisine ouverte avec séjour.
À droite: Le chalet au printemps.

FARRAR RESIDENCE,
PARK CITY, UT, USA

www.bcj.com
Client: Dennis and Vicki Farrar, **Completion:** 2005, **Gross floor area:** 1115 m², **Photos:** Nic Lehoux.

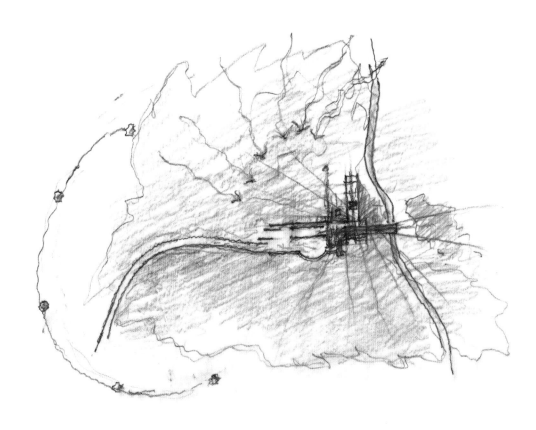

Left: Exterior from below. Links: Außenansicht von unten. À gauche: La maison vue d'en bas. | Right: Sketch. Rechts: Skizze. À droite: Esquisse.

The steep sloping terrain and expansive views to the Wasatch valley were essential in defining the form of the house. Two linear volumes of the guest and master wings slip between the trees and intersect to form the main living space, while also enclosing a private courtyard. The 25-meter lap pool volume continues into the forest; terminating as it cantilevers over a seasonal creek. The material palette complements the natural setting of the house: wood siding, concrete walls, stone masses and expanses of glass create a strong connection to the landscape.

Der steile Geländehang und die weiten Aussichten auf das Wasatch-Tal bestimmten wesentlich die Form des Hauses. Zwei lineare Baukörper mit dem Gäste- und Haupttrakt verlaufen zwischen den Bäumen und überschneiden sich, um den Hauptwohnraum zu bilden, der einen Innenhof umschließt. Das Volumen des 25 Meter langen, schmalen Swimming-pools setzt sich im Wald fort und endet mit einer Auskragung über einem saisonalen Bach. Die Materialpalette ergänzt die natürliche Umgebung des Hauses. Holzverkleidungen, Betonwände, Naturstein und ausgedehnte Glasflächen schaffen eine starke Verbindung zur Landschaft.

Un terrain en pente offrant des vues magnifiques sur la vallée de Wasatch a déterminé l'aspect général de cette maison construite parmi les arbres. Deux volumes linéaires, l'un destiné au propriétaire et l'autre à ses invités, se rejoignent pour former un séjour et une cour intérieure, tandis qu'une piscine couverte de vingt-cinq mètres de long se prolonge jusque dans la forêt, où elle domine un ruisseau intermittent. La palette de matériaux utilisés (murs en pierres et revêtement de bois pour les murs en béton) est en parfaite harmonie avec l'environnement naturel. De vastes surfaces vitrées assurent par ailleurs l'interconnexion entre l'intérieur et le paysage.

Rear view. Rückwärtige Fassade. Face arrière.

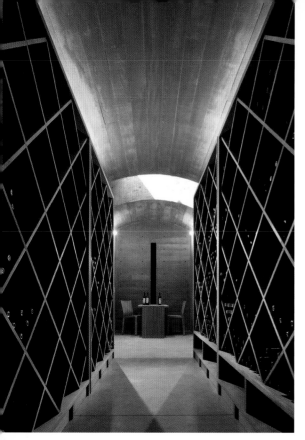

From left to right, from above to below:
Wine cellar, living room, deck, pool.
Right: View of pool from exterior.

Von links nach rechts, von oben nach unten:
Weinkeller, Wohnzimmer, Terrasse, Swimmingpool.
Rechts: Außenansicht.

De gauche à droite, du haut vers le bas:
Cellier, séjour, terrasse, piscine.
À droite: La piscine vue de l'extérieur.

WILDCAT RIDGE RESIDENCE,
SNOWMASS VILLAGE, CO, USA

VOORSANGER ARCHITECTS PC

www.voorsanger.com

Client: Mr. & Mrs. Leon Hirsch, **Completion:** 2004, **Gross floor area:** 1320 m², **Photos:** Thomas Damgaard.

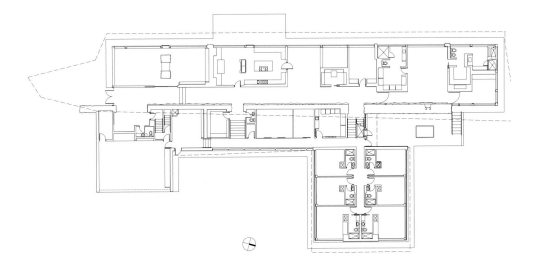

Left: Exterior with glazed façade. Links: Glasfassade. À gauche: Façade entièrement vitrée. | Right: Ground floor plan. Rechts: Grundriss Erdgeschoss. À droite: Plan du rez-de-chaussée..

Designed to accommodate a large family, the house is 61 meters long on its north/south axis, with public spaces oriented to the west and private rooms to the east. Separating those public spaces is a massive stonewall. With ceilings as high as seven meters in some areas, the wall anchors the interiors and contributes a sense of scale. Abundant glass walls frame views of the nearby mountain range. The windows' energy demand is answered by 60 geothermal wells, which provide 100 percent cooling and 95 percent heating for the home. The whole structure is topped by a copper-clad folded-plate roof, which echoes the forms of the mountain range in the distance.

Das für eine große Familie entworfene Haus ist an seiner Nord-Süd-Achse 61 Meter lang. Die gemeinschaftlichen Räume orientieren sich nach Westen, die privaten nach Osten. Eine massive Mauer aus Naturstein trennt die Gemeinschaftszonen voneinander ab. Bei einer Raumhöhe von bis zu sieben Metern verortet die Mauer die Innenräume und unterstützt den Eindruck von Höhe. Ausgedehnte Glaswände rahmen die Aussichten auf die nahe gelegene Bergkette. Den Energiebedarf der Fenster decken 60 Erdwärmebohrungen. Sie sorgen zu 100 Prozent für die Kühlung und zu 95 Prozent für die Beheizung des Hauses. Ein mit Kupfer verkleidetes Faltwerkdach erinnert an die Formen der fernen Berge.

Cette villa orientée nord/sud et conçue pour abriter une famille nombreuse mesure soixante mètres de long. Les pièces communes se trouvent du côté ouest, les chambres face à l'est. Un mur intérieur en pierres d'une hauteur allant jusqu'à 7,30 mètres en certains endroits contribue à l'unification de l'espace. De vastes baies vitrées offrent des vues panoramiques sur les montagnes environnantes. Soixante puits géothermiques couvrent l'intégralité des besoins de climatisation et quatre-vingt-quinze pour cent des besoins de chauffage. Le toit dont les deux pentes évoquent la forme des montagnes voisines est revêtu de plaques de cuivre.

Left: Bird's eye view. Links: Luftbild. Gauche: Vue aérienne. **Right**: Rear view. Rechts: Rückansicht. À droite: Face arrière.

From left to right, from above to below:
Shower, study, driveway view.
Right: Hallway with stone wall.

Von links nach rechts, von oben nach unten:
Dusche, Arbeitsplatz, Auffahrt.
Rechts: Flur mit massiver Steinwand.

De gauche à droite, du haut vers le bas:
Salle de bain, bureau, auvent de la zone d'entrée.
À droite: Couloir et mur en pierres.

HILLER RESIDENCE,
WINTER PARK, CO, USA

MICHAEL P. JOHNSON DESIGN STUDIOS

www.mpjstudio.com
Client: Ruth Hiller, **Completion:** 2005, **Gross floor area:** 278 m², **Photos:** Bill Timmerman.

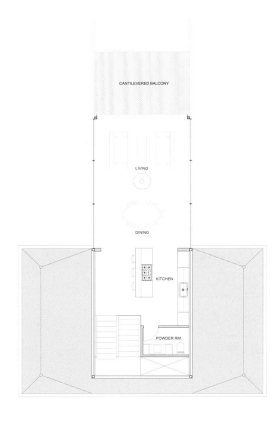

Left: General view at night. Links: Gesamtansicht. À gauche: La maison la nuit. | Right: Floor plan. Rechts: Grundriss. À droite: Plan.

Ruth Hiller approached Michael P. Johnson Design Studios Ltd. with the challenge to remodel a poorly designed building in a manner within a minimalist design ethic. With little to work with it was suggested that the existing residence be removed and relocated elsewhere. Working with the existing basement foundation a two-story solution allowed the living, dining, and kitchen to fly above the dense evergreen forest. The lower level contains two master bedroom suites, entry and a commons room. The basement was designated for use as a painting studio with natural light borrowed by the use of light wells located on the west elevation.

Ruth Hiller wandte sich an Michael P. Johnson Design Studios Ltd. mit der schwierigen Aufgabe, ein unzulänglich entworfenes Gebäude in einer minimalistischen Designethik umzubauen. Aufgrund des dürftigen Bestands wurde vorgeschlagen, das bestehende Wohnhaus zu demontieren und zu versetzen. Über der vorhandenen Kellergründung entstanden zwei Geschosse, sodass der Wohn- und Essbereich sowie die Küche über dem Nadelwald schweben. In der unteren Ebene befinden sich zwei Hauptschlafräume, der Eingang und ein Aufenthaltsraum. Das Kellergeschoss ist für ein Maleratelier konzipiert, das über Lichtschächte an der Westfassade mit natürlichem Licht versorgt wird.

La propriétaire a tout d'abord chargé les architectes de réaménager en style minimaliste un bâtiment préexistant. Mais celui-ci s'est révélé être de si piètre qualité, qu'il a bientôt été décidé de ne conserver que les fondations. Le nouveau bâtiment comprend un rez-de-chaussée qui abrite le vestibule, deux chambres et une pièce commune, ainsi qu'un niveau supérieur où la cuisine, le séjour et la salle à manger semblent flotter au-dessus de la forêt de sapins environnante. Le percement de puits de lumière du côté ouest a par ailleurs permis d'aménager un studio de peintre au sous-sol.

View from below. Blick von unten. La villa vue d'en bas.

From left to right, from above to below:
Bedroom, kitchen, bathroom, entrance area.
Right: Living room with fireplace.

Von links nach rechts, von oben nach unten:
Schlafzimmer, Küche, Badezimmer, Eingangsbereich.
Rechts: Wohnzimmer mit Kamin.

De gauche à droite, du haut vers le bas:
Chambre, cuisine ouverte, salle de bain, vestibule.
À droite: Séjour avec cheminée.

Imprint
The Deutsche Nationalbibliothek lists this publication in the Deutsche
Nationalbibliografie; detailed bibliographical data are available on
the internet at http://dnb.d-nb.de.

ISBN 978-3-03768-021-6

© 2010 by Braun Publishing AG
www.braun-publishing.ch

1st edition 2010

Translation: Marcel Saché (French version), Cosima Talhouni (English),
Joanna Zajac-Heinken (German)
Text editing: Michelle Galindo (English)
Graphic concept and layout: Michaela Prinz